T0150721

ROBERT DUNCAN
In San Francisco

ROBERT DUNCAN
In San Francisco

Michael Rumaker

With an Interview & Letters
Edited by Ammiel Alcalay and Megan Paslawski

CITY LIGHTS / GREY FOX
San Francisco

Library of Congress Cataloging-in-Publication Data
Rumaker, Michael, 1932–
  Robert Duncan in San Francisco / Michael Rumaker ; edited by Ammiel Alcalay & Megan Paslawski ; with letters & an interview.
    p. cm.
  ISBN 978-0-87286-590-7
1. Duncan, Robert Edward, 1919-1988—Homes and haunts—California—San Francisco. 2. Rumaker, Michael, 1932—Friends and associates. 3. Gay men—California—San Francisco—Biography. 4. Poets, American—20th century—Biography. 5. San Francisco (Calif.)—Intellectual life—20th century. 6. San Francisco (Calif.)—Biography. I. Alcalay, Ammiel. II. Paslawski, Megan. III. Title.

PS3507.U629Z88 2012
811'.54—dc23
[B]

                      2012036019

City Lights Books are published at the City Lights Bookstore
261 Columbus Avenue, San Francisco, CA 94133
www.citylights.com

Contents

Introduction *vii*

Chapter One *3*

Chapter Two *21*

Chapter Three *65*

Selected Letters
Michael Rumaker / Robert Duncan *85*

An Interview with Michael Rumaker *111*

Introduction

"THE WHOLE THING HAS NO MEANING IF IT IS NOT SIGNED"

When Robert Duncan was twenty-five—only a year older than Michael Rumaker would be when Black Mountain College asked Duncan to serve as Rumaker's external examiner—he published "The Homosexual in Society" in the August 1944 issue of Dwight Macdonald's magazine *Politics*. The article was short, but it was seen as momentous because it issued from someone who openly acknowledged that he was part of the human race.

Just three months before the appearance of Duncan's article, Charles Olson resigned from his position at the Office of War Information. His resignation bore witness to deep policy changes that would lead the United States to assume the mantle and practice of imperial might. While the US took the role of global steward and policeman, its government-sponsored cultural policy would conspire with economic and military policy. The very framework of knowledge would alter radically with the growth of the university and the culture industry in the Cold War.

In August 1945, less than two weeks after the US dropped atomic bombs on Hiroshima and Nagasaki, Olson changed the narrative of *Call Me Ishmael*, his groundbreaking study of Melville, to focus on the tragic story of the whale-ship Essex, on which the crew resorted to cannibalism after going astray. His own change of course away from party politics left Olson to seek a new base of knowledge and experience from which to explore what Duncan would later call "the underbelly of the nation."

Michael Rumaker was born into this "underbelly" in 1932, but would journey from it to one base of new knowledge, Black Mountain College. With Olson as Rector, Duncan as teacher, and Rumaker as student, the paths of these three men aligned in their search for new ways of writing and being.

Rumaker was one of nine children born into a working-class Catholic family who struggled to make ends meet during the Depression. Rumaker's mother, as he wrote in *Black Mountain Days*, "helped pay for her keep and my getting born by peeling potatoes in the kitchen of the Retreat, a maternity home for poor married women of 'good moral standing.'" The circumstances of this childhood would loom large in Rumaker's most ambitious novel *Pagan Days* (1999), narrated in the first person by Mickey Lithwack as he grows from six to nine years old. Were it not for Olson's instinctive recognition of East Coast working class boys as his spiritual kin, Rumaker might have seemed on this evidence an unlikely candidate for Black Mountain.

Between the poles of *Pagan Days*, which named and celebrated his own queer beginnings, and his earliest stories (written at Black Mountain in the mid-1950s and shrouded in the depths of unconscious impulse), Rumaker's work distinguished itself by what Duncan later characterized as "a writing that matters, that feeds a hunger for depth of experience and that will make new demands upon our understanding of human life."

Few writers in this country have explored the politics of memory as profoundly as Rumaker. His understanding of memory was a hard-won product of years in which he found himself silenced, first institutionalized for two years at the Rockland Psychiatric Center and later choked off by alcohol and drugs. *The Butterfly*, an account of Rumaker's post-Rockland relationship with Yoko Ono, painfully limned the effort it took to break that silence. The book's appearance in 1962 and the publication of *Gringos and Other Stories* in 1967 were the last the wider world heard from Rumaker for ten years, until the publication of *A Day and a Night at the Baths*, a groundbreaking portrait of sexual freedom powered by gay liberation. Allen Ginsberg joyously declared that *Baths* allowed him to see through Rumaker's "eyes and feel thru his body."

Rumaker's silence through the late '60s and early '70s matched Duncan's in intensity and perhaps in inspiration, despite how differently they expressed their malaise. In 1968, Robert Duncan declared that he would not publish a new collection for fifteen years. By the time Rumaker started working on his portrait of Duncan in San Francisco, Duncan was a poet of major stature whom few knew and even fewer could read, given that he deliberately removed himself from the careerist gravy-train. By circulating his work among friends and in very limited editions, Duncan could block out a wider but narrower world and discover what poetry asked of him. Across the country in Nyack, NY, Rumaker was learning to bring the same focus and strength to his own writing, though his journey required him to publish.

Some critics, cleverer writers than readers, have described *Robert Duncan in San Francisco* as *Michael Rumaker in San Francisco*. Such an interpretation ignores the generosity of the book: a generosity that acknowledges the influence and spiritual guidance one person, however unconsciously, can communicate to those around him. The memoir repays Rumaker's debt to Duncan and the other mentors who helped Rumaker survive San Francisco of the 1950s, a city where queers congregated only to find themselves kettled by police, mainstream society, and their own fear. But as in all great writing, this debt was not simply to individuals, no matter how cherished they might be, but to the act of writing itself, to the historical and political process of exploring how identity is formed through perception of oneself and of oneself through others, in specific times and places, through specific forms, and in the context of very specific oppression. *Robert Duncan in San Francisco*, to remain true to Duncan's liberationist instincts, must be the story of many, all connected in their struggle to live more truly: Rumaker hiding in his clerk's uniform at parties, the painter Tom Field opening his home to all passersby, poet John Wieners shocking his landlord with his cherry lipstick.

Back on the East Coast after a year and a half in San Francisco, Rumaker wrote Duncan about some poems of his that appeared in *Measure*, the magazine edited by Wieners. "Your 'Propositions' in Measure is . . . I can't find the word. I'm thrilled, and moved. You're the richest man in San Francisco." Rumaker located the wellspring of Duncan's richness in his careful construction of a protective domestic space in which he practiced the freedom that he then brought into the outer world.

Because he fought for so long to feel comfortable in his own queer skin, Rumaker took years to understand the import of his encounters with Duncan on Duncan's home ground, where the poet found spiritual nourishment through a loving relationship with the great artist Jess Collins. As Rumaker later explained, "I didn't know the secret then: the more open, the more protected you are."

Rumaker had at last understood the precept that Duncan had stated so clearly in 1944, when he castigated the notion of group allegiance and its consequences. To hold the "devotion to human freedom, toward the liberation of human love," he wrote, "every written word, every spoken word, every action, every purpose must be examined and considered. The old fears, the old specialties will be there, mocking and tempting; the old protective associations will be there, offering for a surrender of one's humanity congratulations upon one's special nature and value. It must always be recognized that those who have surrendered their humanity, are not less than oneself."

Such thinking, as Duncan wrote back in response to Dwight Macdonald's well-founded trepidation for Duncan's public future were he to publish "The Homosexual in Society," must be backed by openness: "it is only by my committing myself openly that the belief and the desire of others for an open and free discussion of homosexual problems may be encouraged . . . *the whole thing has no meaning if it is not signed.*"

This faith in openness and dislike of in-groups would temper Duncan's sometimes contrary politics through the 1960s, as when he described the humanity of the police charging demonstrators at a march on the Pentagon where he had been scheduled to speak: "Two of the faces I find immovable with hatred for what I am. What have they been told I am? But the third wavers in the commanding panic and pleads with his eyes, Retreat, retreat, do not make me have to encounter you."

This encounter made Duncan realize that he must refuse an audience that would want what they think he can give them: "In the face of an overwhelming audience waiting for me to dare move them, I would speak to those alike in soul, I know not who or where they are. But I have only the language of our commonness, alive with them as well as me, the speech of the audience in its refusal in which I would come into that confidence. The poem in which my heart beats speaks like to unlike, kind to unkind. The line of the poem itself confronts me where I must volunteer my love, and I saw, long before this war, wrath move in that music that troubles me."

Such contradictory motivation—and such openness to it—has made Duncan's work, like Rumaker's, extremely difficult to mobilize on behalf of any single identity and thus more difficult for the critical establishment to assess. The appearance of Duncan's *H.D. Book*, along with Lisa Jarnot's biography and the first volume of Duncan's *Collected Writings*, parallels the publication and republication of key works by and about Rumaker: this book, *Black Mountain Days*, *A Day and a Night at the Baths*, *Selected Letters*, and Leverett T. Smith Jr.'s *Eroticizing the Nation: Michael Rumaker's Fiction*. All point to a revival of interest that might further the possibility of these essential writers once again circulating more widely and re-inhabiting the common currency of significant historical and literary achievement. Our aim in presenting this new edition of Michael Rumaker's *Robert Duncan in San Francisco* is to provide a new context for the work, both through an interview we conducted with Rumaker in February 2012, and the publication of selected correspondence between him and Duncan. In doing so, this text illustrates an evolving relationship that reveals obscured lives—particularly queer lives—at the height of the Cold War. These new and newly gathered materials challenge the historical categories, whether of schools or identities, we have received. We may instead follow the journeys these people took to see where they lead.

Ammiel Alcalay & Megan Paslawski

For Tom Field, in loving memory

ROBERT DUNCAN IN SAN FRANCISCO

One

Robert Duncan wrote me several letters from Black Mountain College in North Carolina in the summer of 1956, saying he wanted to come to Philadelphia (where I was living after graduating) to meet me. Because of various unexpected changes in plans, we didn't get to meet til late summer of that year.

Duncan hitchhiked up from Black Mountain and arrived at my basement apartment at 21st and Spruce on a Saturday morning. The first thing of course, were his eyes, those curious and lovely eyes that looked at me, directly, while in the same instant, with hesitancy and vulnerability, looked around me and off to the sides. He was nervously casing me and, simultaneously, what lay beyond the door. Voluptuously plumpish, with a coxcomb of dark hair, he stepped into the room. Shy with each other at first, he began to talk, nonstop, generating energy for a dozen people, radiant with intelligence and enthusiasm. In a word, overwhelming, like a force of nature. His presence filled the room. (Charles Olson once said, "Duncan's like a roman candle, dazzling and exciting for the first couple hours, then it begins to wear you out. You want to go away, or you want *him* to go away—go home and write it down." This from a man not exactly lacking in overwhelming razzle-dazzle himself.)

It was a bad time to meet Duncan because I was drinking too much and spending nights cruising Rittenhouse Square. I was working in a financial advertising agency during the day (Black Mountain had prepared me for nothing but my destiny, but in spite of that I bluffed my way into getting hired for a job I knew nothing about). I was trying to write at night but didn't have the concentration and energy I'd had at Black Mountain, or the sense of protection. I was also "in love."

I'd met a young man, a writing student, when I went back to the college for a week's vacation-visit in the first week of August 1956. Duncan was away at that time so I didn't get to meet him then. The young man told me he was 18th in line for the throne of England. He also believed himself to be the reincarnation of Holden Caulfield, said he even had the typewriter that *Catcher in the Rye* was written on. It didn't matter. He was slender and blond and wore black-rimmed glasses that enhanced his good looks. He was also heavily into pot and pills, especially speed and barbiturates, as were some of the few remaining students at the college. This was near the final closing of the school and in the year since I'd left there was a drastic change. There was a psychotic, unpredictable energy in the air. Jerry van de Wiele, the painter, told me that when certain students came to visit, when he was living at Last Chance on the road to the farm, he was careful to put the axe he used for cutting firewood in a safe place, out of sight and reach.

During my stay, Olson and Betty Kaiser, with whom he was now living after first wife Connie's departure, invited me up to supper one night and Charles gleefully told me (but with a touch of bewilderment and exasperation in his voice since the quality of the work of what writing students there were had dropped considerably) that the remaining faculty should vote to take down the Black Mountain College sign over the Gatehouse entrance and "run up a bright red flag that says 'SECONAL' on it in big letters!"

What seemed the main, and singularly constructive, activity of that spring quarter (Duncan's *Medea* was done in the summer of 1956) had been the production of Robert's farce *The Origins of Old Son*, with a cast that involved practically the entire population of the school. Van de Wiele told me he had felt uncomfortable playing the baby, in baby hat and dress, his legs hanging out of the carriage, because he strongly suspected Duncan's baby was Olson and that Olson suspected it too, although Charles didn't say anything about it. Jerry knew, however, that set look Olson could get that spoke loud and clear.

Charles had introduced us to Duncan's poetry in his writing classes. He would read us the latest work he'd received in letters from Duncan out in San Francisco or, later, in Mallorca, and we'd discuss the poems. Charles' own energetic affection for the poems was, as with so much else that grabbed him, contagious.

Once he said in a writing class after reading a new poem Duncan had sent him, "It's like Duncan has no 'social sense' in his poems. The lines of them drop down—They're all movement" and here he lifted his long arms high over his

head and let them drop slowly in a shimmering motion—
"Like falling bolts of silk."

When Duncan arrived that Saturday morning it had been, despite our correspondence, abruptly and without much advance notice. The trouble was I had planned that weekend to be with my writing-student friend who had since left Black Mountain and was now living in New York City. I told Robert this and that I felt bad leaving him alone in a cellar apartment in a strange city.

He said he planned to stay til Monday anyway; too, he wanted to see the Arensberg Collection again at the Philadelphia Museum, that he could amuse himself while I was gone, and was gracious enough to tell me not to worry about him, we'd talk when I got back on Sunday.

I don't remember that weekend in New York at all except for walking late into the Cedar Bar with my friend. For several hours previously we'd been smoking and popping pills and drinking. I went eventually into a blackout and awakened from it for a few moments as we walked to the crowded rear of the bar. Several people I knew were there from Black Mountain, Joel Oppenheimer, Fee Dawson, Dan Rice. As I moved down the long narrow bar to the back, each looked at me with a set face and then parted, moved several steps away, making way for me. I can only imagine what I looked like from the expression in their eyes, as if they were looking at a stranger, and someone they didn't want to get close to.

When I returned to Philly Sunday afternoon I was jittery and exhausted. I wished Robert wasn't there. This nonstop talking cyclone of energy was more than I could handle in my hungover, strung-out state. I have said that this was a bad time to meet this poet whose work I esteemed but whose personal life frightened the bejesus out of me. For Robert was unabashedly and openly queer at a time when practically everybody in America from Senator Joe McCarthy on up was a terminal closet case.

After three years at Black Mountain I'd learned how to write but I was still pretty callow about a lot of things. Love in particular, and gay love most emphatically. Same-sex relations at the college were tacitly approved but never openly discussed, at least not as comfortably by faculty and students as non-gay relationships. The prevailing attitude was tolerance (no small thing at the time; given the climate of the decade, even in the relatively protected enclave of Black Mountain, care had to be taken since Buncombe County was most definitely a part of the USA). Charles' remark to me in the early 1950s in one of the few brief times he ever discussed gayness that "there are no camps" was the only sensible words I'd heard on sexuality up til then.

So here was a real faggot, open and reasonably happy about it, unafraid to be what he was. It frightened me. I, who had so carefully striven to appear "straight" in my job and in the city of my birth, crowded with working-class Catholic relatives. It was only after a quart or two of Schmidt's ("of Philadelphia") that I had the courage to cruise Rittenhouse Square. A number of times I was beaten and robbed, three times in my basement apartment, once by two men who drove me to a dump in South Philly. Once raped, twice almost murdered. Each time by homophobic men, as I always found out too late, posing as upfront gays. I went to them because "straight-appearing" was more attractive than "gay appearing," more desirable because accepted as the "healthier." I was halved by the split of that ignorance.

I only wanted Robert to go away (but for different reasons than Charles had sometimes wished), this gay man who I'd heard early on at Black Mountain was living, and had been living for some years in San Francisco, with another man, a painter named Jess, in what, from what I could learn, was a reasonably harmonious and loving friendship. That seemed unbelievable to me. At Black Mountain I'd lived for a time with another student who was gay and even though everyone knew this they pretended not to. The student and I couldn't be open and comfortable in our situation with others, and, aside from our own personal abrasions, that sense of being not quite permissible affected our own feelings for each other. To be tolerated isn't the same as sharing an equal and open acceptance. Black Mountain in the 1950s, for all its latitude in other areas, reflected in microcosm the general attitudes of American society at large, and that was that ungay was more okay than gay, and that gay, no matter the liberal solicitude, didn't somehow fit. Mainly there was, for me, and the other gay males and lesbians at the college, no source of identity to plug into. However, considering what lay outside the Gatehouse then, at Black Mountain you could at least breathe and, most importantly, you weren't hassled for being what you were. Uppermost, the spirit of acceptance was for all, in the work being done there, open and "rough around the edges" as Charles said Black Mountain should always be.

Robert told me he had amused himself by reading some of my personal stuff while I was gone (perhaps unconsciously he was still playing the part of my outside examiner). In my exacerbated state that really pissed me off. But I kept silent. That wasn't the real reason for my anger.

When it was time to go to bed we split the bed apart (it was a small apartment and I had one of those narrow Hollywood jobs, secondhand). Can't remember who slept on the mattress on the floor. Being the typical young egoist and hypocrite, I was afraid Robert would put the make on me and I couldn't respond—and, more likely, unconsciously afraid he wouldn't. I had glimpsed the recognition of something in my own face in his eyes and had looked away. His eyes were a hand-mirror to mine. He was the bountiful looker. But my own seeking then was niggardly, pinched, cataracted and only sexual.

My initial, and romantic, sense of him was that Robert was like some sensuous flower, all-enfolding, too heavily perfumed. I ran from the pull of its fascination. Its ecstatic brilliance hurt the eyes, in his person, in his poems. Strange and unknown to me, I dreaded its power. How could I know then that what seemed so fearful and alien was as natural as breath? That it was the center and secret of all happiness?

I left for work in the morning relieved to know that when I got home in the evening Robert would be gone.

Beginning in 1954, as a writing student at Black Mountain College, I had sent several of my early short stories, at the urging of Charles Olson, to Robert Creeley in Palma de Mallorca where he was then living with his family and editing the first issues of *The Black Mountain Review*. Creeley liked the stories and showed them to Robert Duncan who was also at that time staying in Mallorca with Jess Collins. Because Duncan responded with excitement and favor to the work, especially "The Pipe" and "Exit 3," when it came time for my graduation, in 1955, Olson, backed by Creeley, decided Duncan would be an excellent choice to act as outside examiner. "We don't want any academic types," Olson had said.

There was a sticky moment or two when Duncan, understandably uncertain as to just what was expected of him in the matter, did, in part, ask questions of my range and ability as a writer in a somewhat academic vein. Still, the concerns and generosity of the person were evident in the letter he wrote to Creeley (who was now teaching at the college) and, by extension, to the Black Mountain faculty, from Bañalbufar on October 7, 1955 as a clarification after I had graduated.

I quote it here for that reason and for the record, and also for the sense of Robert's stance and thought at the time, and not for his generous praise, heartening as it was:

Dear Bob:

You ask me to consider this work of Mike Rumaker's "with reference to its level, educationally speaking"; "does he write as competently, and as potentially well, as the average graduate from the usual college?" There need be no qualifications of my answer that he does indeed do as well as the better than average graduate from a college. In the short story, in such pieces as "The Pipe" or "Exit Three" [sic], Rumaker has, after all, a professional command of his craft and is engaged in that craft at a level which is to be compared not with "the average graduate" but with the best at work in the field. One has only to compare an earlier story "Loie's Party" or "The Jest" to appreciate what has been learned—and in the terms of learning as well as command, in the terms of gain in craft which I take it comes from his engagement in learning as well as in terms of his command which I take comes from his engagement in the immediate task of the writing at the time of writing, he is certainly at the best level of graduate writing.

From the three critical pieces provided for my consideration, it is clear that Rumaker's work in this type of essay is better than average, certainly as good as average graduate work. The papers[1] are casual, not academic—but it is a difference of task set, not a difference of competence in organization and craft that would distinguish here. And the insights, the constant interplay of experience and new materials which is of the essence of a critical intelligence—these are here, as they are not often to be found in graduating students at the "A" level.

Yours truly,
(signed)
Robert Duncan

I would also like to quote, again, as a basis for this reminiscence and for the record, and to establish that personal sense of his kindness and caring, from part of a letter

Duncan wrote to me from Black Mountain, where he was now teaching, on March 30, 1956, several months before our first meeting. The quote is to give the value of the person and poet Duncan was, and is, not only to myself in my apprentice writing days, but to other young writers as well. It's to give, too, his perception of the different angles in which each of us approached our writing:

> They put me in a hot position by #graduating# you. I would not myself like to be "graduated" as a writer. What does it mean? Anyway, Creeley pickd me because he knew I liked your work—this means that I read it in the same sense that I read anything, because it feeds me. And how to get that across? It isn't anyway part of my recommendation. What does it mean that you write well, which is easy to say, and sets me up to discriminate? when it is a pleasure I get, it is the life of all conversations, all talk in your stories . . . and then the veracity that lingers. EXIT THREE still stays with me after six months . . . tho I forget sometimes and think it was something that happened to me when I was hitch hiking. You invade my own experience that way. But I must be the strangest of audiences for you . . . you are so straight. And I glamor-enamored. Well, I am used to arriving at my soul's home in some monstrosity of history, some Venice . . . but just so, I am amazed at where you get on a truck, a pipe, or a highway. THE RIVER and the poems I have not read yet. If, when I read the poems, there is

anything I feel right to say I will write you. But the damnd difficulty of my position in having to write an official recommendation was that I view this thing about a writer, a real writer as unofficial . . . one ought to FLUNK it into its own authenticity. The point about the What about Henry James? was just that I couldnt see you (and, thats the point, cant) as the product of a school. It was not as that but because one saw too that "graduation" meant jobs perhaps etc. But you belong in my heart as a reader in your own place. Not as a comment on H.J. or J.J. or even Robert Creeley. Oh well, tho Mark Twain and Dostoyevsky do come to mind somehow. And I think you would get a bang out of reading Chekov's BLACK MONK, tho I dont know why. It hasnt got the genius of talk. But I'm write, right, here—you aren't just the genius of talk. The pit on one side for you is the "camp," the folk-ways of the queer—just as for me it is the "drag," exotic decor of the queer. But the human being is more important so far to you—this is what I get out of your writing—than any of his minorities. And I always find men there, they're all parts of a Man. And that I think is the firmest hold I have on your work. Your beautiful sense of man's nature. . . .

When I graduated from Black Mountain College in 1955 I planned to give myself a year in Philadelphia to work and pay off some small debts. Luckily, I was able to stay with some friends in the small top floor room of their tiny 18th-century, three-story Father-Son-and-Holy-Ghost house, as those old servant houses are called, on back alley St. James Street in Center City, while I looked for work and could finally rent the basement apartment at 21st & Spruce (where another visitor, John Wieners, stopped by one day but didn't stay long, Beantown chauvinist to the core, opining, "Philadelphia was trying too hard to be like Boston").

I had also met a wealthy lesbian, and all her lesbian friends, who lived around the corner on Locust Street in a much more luxurious apartment, and who was in analysis to make her stop being a lesbian—a quite common barbaric practice in those days and with whom I on occasion slept to help create the miracle, and with whom I drank her Black & White Scotch and listened to the smoky-voiced Chris Connor, especially her queer-popular "Lush Life."

When the miracle didn't occur she would rush off in ever more avid appetite, still a miraculously intact dyke, to the arms of one of her women friends.

Having had a student deferment for four years I also had to take care of my draft status. (At my induction examination, after several minutes of indecision, I checked the question "Have you had any homosexual experiences?" with a Yes, and became 4-F.) In October 1956, shortly after Robert's visit, the year was up, my debts paid off and the Selective Service no longer a threat. I left Philly and hitchhiked to San Francisco. Shortly before setting out Robert, who was now back in San Francisco, wrote:

> . . . Yes, you can send your things care of me at this
> address [1137 DeHaro]. Where we will find a place

for you to stay is still up in the air. When I got your letter I phoned Tom Field who was looking for a place himself—but I haven't seen him since. If that workd out, it might be the easiest for you but how-ever it goes I think I can find a corner of this city ready for you when you arrive. . . .

I thought it would be a good place to start again, a place totally unknown and new to me, 3,000 miles away from the placid brick of Philadelphia and the magnetic pull of Rittenhouse Square dangers and addictions. Also, some friends from Black Mountain had gone there just before the closing of the school. In a different place maybe I would get to know Duncan in a different way.

With nothing more than $30 in my pocket and clutch-ing my mother's old battered suitcase, my lesbian friend drove me, in style at least, in her cream-colored Mercedes-Benz convertible to the Valley Forge entrance of the Pennsylvania Turnpike early one morning in October 1956 to begin my hitchhiking across the continent. After a day or two of numerous hops, in Vandalia, Illinois (curiously, where Abe Lincoln began practicing law and later the loca-tion of the writing farm where James Jones wrote *From Here to Eternity*), I luckily got a lift with an Air Force jet pilot who was headed for the outskirts of San Francisco. A pleas-ant enough guy who talked about the girl he'd left behind in Indianapolis the whole trip but who didn't mind shar-ing a bed with me at several of our overnight stops, aptly enough at one place in Oklahoma called the Homotel, the young, attractive pilot saying to the desk clerk, "A double bed's OK." A fast driver, we made it to Needles, California, in three days. Near San Francisco, he dropped me off where I could get a bus to Buchanan Street where Tom Field and Paul Alexander, both painters and former Black Mountain students, now shared an apartment and where they'd invited me to stay til I got a place of my own. As I waited for the McAllister Street bus the first thing that struck me about the city was the look of the police on motorcycles. They were dressed in white crash helmets, black leather jackets and jodhpurs with stout black boots, and had bullets and hardware bundled around their middles. You must remember that this police dress was not so common as it is now. They made me think of the SS men in anti-Nazi propaganda movies during World War II. It certainly made me uneasy.

I was to learn in my year and a half stay in San Francisco that it was indeed a police city. There was, in spite of the extraordinary quality of light over the city, a heavy climate of fear, not so much from the violence which occurred, although there was enough of that, but rather from the activities and presence of the police themselves. This was particularly true for gay men. There was also the burgeoning narcotics squad with the beginnings of the wider use of drugs. But the Morals Squad was everywhere and the entrapment of gay males in the streets, the parks and in numerous public places was a constant fear and common occurrence. Often the most handsome, hung, desirable-looking cops were used for these plainclothes operations. I often wondered who did the selecting.

My first night in San Francisco Paul Alexander took me to Lafayette Park on Pacific Heights (Tom was working nightwork and unable to be there when I arrived) and showed me the view of the city looking off toward Telegraph Hill and Russian Hill, and Marin County across the bay. Looking out at the vast downward run of lights from that height and smelling the cold-salt smell of the Pacific in the darkness, I knew, just as I had several years earlier in my first days visiting Black Mountain, this was the place I needed to be.

We walked to North Beach to The Place, which had been opened (like The Tin Angel[2]) by former Black Mountain students, the painters Leo Krikorian and Knute Stiles. The huge dark wooden bar, elaborately and intricately carved, with fluted glass lamps set between its columns and large, faded mirrors, had been found in some old saloon long gone out of business. It was one of those antique bars carved in New York City, I was told, and brought around Cape Horn by ship to San Francisco before the turn of the century, like most wood products and timber to that craftsman-sparse and sparsely wooded area of California.

Paul introduced me to steam beer (The Place had only a beer and wine license) and we weren't seated at the bar more than a few minutes when the door burst open and a horde of people rushed in, young men and women shouting and laughing. "Ginsberg for President!" they were hollering, over and over, as they ran around the bar and up onto the balcony at the rear and back down again. There was a loose, good-natured feeling in their highjinks and roughhousing. A few ran around and hugged and kissed acquaintances sitting at the bar or at tables.

I asked Paul what was going on. He said Allen Ginsberg had just given a reading that night of *Howl* some place in

North Beach. These celebrants, with their spontaneous energy and boisterous camaraderie, were something new to me. The Place was so crowded with them I'm not certain if Ginsberg was there himself that night. I found out later he and Peter Orlovsky left the city shortly after for Tangiers, after confiscation of the City Lights edition of *Howl* by United States Customs, and I didn't get to meet them both until 1958 in New York.[3]

But I was delighted; perplexed, too. This rough energy was something new in the air. That was my first introduction to North Beach where, it turned out, all the main action was.

But action was wherever Robert Duncan was. Robert lived with Jess Collins in a large comfortable apartment in a gray frame house on Potrero Hill, the old Russian section of the city. The walls were hung with paintings by Jess and others, and lined with bookshelves built by Jess for the apartment. There was a small desk Robert used only for writing letters. In the bathroom you could read Jess' cutup and reassembled Dick Tracy comic strips, mounted on the wall over the toilet, while you pissed. The apartment was filled with an abundance and pleasant disorder of beloved objects. I felt comfortable there. It was like a shelter against all that was around it.

Jess was thin and shy, a pallor like someone who stays indoors a lot. Quiet-spoken, when he did speak, he seemed like a vulnerable and sickly adolescent, although he was then in his 30s. He delivered mail at Christmas, and any other odd jobs he could find, to help put food on the table and pay the rent. Robert was assistant to Ruth Witt-Diamant at the Poetry Center (he was instrumental in getting poets like Olson and Denise Levertov to read there), but had taken typing jobs in the past to help run the household. (Olson, when he learned of this, said one night in a writing class at Black Mountain, "A poet of Duncan's stature having to do *typing* to make a *living!*" in outrage and disbelief.)

When people came to visit Robert, Jess stayed in his room, his presence felt more strongly in the awareness of his being just beyond the next wall.

Robert, who could be strongly outspoken and not always careful of the feelings of others, even his friends, was careful with Jess. He treated and spoke of him the way one does with something valuable. I saw that Jess was necessary to Robert. He was like a steady and determined presence Duncan could always return to.

Often, unprepared to handle so many uncertainties in my own life, over-excited and often over-confused in a new city, it was agreeable to think of Robert with Jess up on Potrero Hill, at home, busy and protected. After reading one of his new poems I mailed Robert a note and said he was the richest man in San Francisco. And he was. He was so open-eyed. I didn't know the secret then: the more open, the more protected you are; have more surface space to deflect, to receive; are more supple and defended. Pinched in on myself, after my experiences in Philadelphia, hunched in uncertainty, I was an easy target, a pushover, in such shrunk space.

I liked to think of Jess as the grounding in Duncan's reach, in his work and his needs, in a city which was then, for me, permeated with the shrinkage of conformity and repression.

Paradoxically, I also sensed that the openness that emanated from Potrero Hill was akin to the open energy I felt in The Place the night of Ginsberg's reading of *Howl*. A new vitality was beginning to stir in the light and spaciously open air of the city in spite of the rigidity that was everywhere. It seemed that everybody was writing and painting and making music. Dress, hair, talk was shaggier, rawer; fresh idioms of speech were possible. To me, the look and talk of those most actively involved was like an extension and coalescence of earlier Black Mountain changearounds that had cohered and emerged simultaneously in Swannanoa Valley and the Bay Area. Jazz was all over the place and poets were reading their poems to it. Speech and manner got quirkier, the surprise of variance and singular eccentricity was everywhere in North Beach. It was a haven and matrix for the possible, as was that other center, Potrero Hill. San Francisco was very much Robert Duncan's city. His presence was everywhere. If Ginsberg had been forced temporarily into exile by the authorities, Duncan was still very much in place.

Two

FAST TAKES:

Robert reading: His voice ecstatic with an electricity of feeling, the pages trembling in his hand; his head, body, quivering as he read the poem. Robust as he was, his body looked, in those moments, too small and frail a thing to contain the intense energy of the words he was speaking. It was as if an immense incandescence sprang charged from his flesh, as if he were struggling to contain it. It burst from him and with such force I, sitting in the audience, even at that distance, was afraid it would break him, that his physical self would rip apart at any moment if the poem went on much longer.

Robert's dress at that time could be described as "California Poet Casual." Unlike the tight work jeans, faded blue work shirt, black turtleneck sweater, stevedore sock hat, high-laced work shoes and leather jacket that was poet Jack Spicer's only outfit and made him look like any longshoreman on the Embarcadero, Robert wore full-sleeved shirts of soft material with broad collars in earth as well as bright pastel colors. He particularly favored, for parties and readings, a wide purple tie with the fattest Windsor knot I'd ever seen. A bright orange tie and a pink one were also worn, but not as often. On occasion he'd tie a large, loose fluffy poet's bow around his neck which enhanced his usual jaunty and cocky air. His trousers always seemed baggy and nondescript, mostly of a dark color, brown, not unlike most of the cuts and shades of trousers worn by men in the 1950s, with their wide legs and cuffs and a bolt of cloth in the crotch when you sat down. Levis and workshirts were becoming the standard garb of the younger writers and artists (as they had been at Black Mountain) in what seemed an unconscious throw-back and direct reconnection to Whitman—Ginsberg, for instance, dressed like a working stiff; Kerouac like the rail-road brakeman he was; Robert Creeley like a Basque peasant. The wearing of tight levis and pipestem trousers was the emergence of a wonderful strut and show of the body below the navel.

No matter what he had on there was always a touch of the dandy about Duncan, even in huaraches and a Mexican peasant's blouse, or in an old pullover worn against the San Francisco fog and damp. In his gestures, his walk, the saucy cock of his head with its brash combed up pompadour, there was a delightful aura of the fop. Although I don't remember him wearing any jewelry, there were times when his sensu-ous fingers seemed covered with rings set with curious and dazzling jewels.

Sitting across from Duncan at a table up in the balco-ny of The Place. Duncan, having had a few unaccustomed steam beers (he didn't drink that much), folded his arms on the table, leaned over close and looked at me slit-eyed, became a Spaniard. "I need glamor," he said.

From one of the countless jobs advertised in the *Chronicle* and *Examiner*, a good time for job hunting, applying for a clerk's job at tall, gray Pacific Gas & Electric down in the financial district. The affable blond personnel manager looking over my application was pleased to see I was a college graduate (I let him think Black Mountain was your run-of-the-mill small Southern liberal arts college) but wanted to know why I was 4-F. I knew if I told him I was queer I certainly wouldn't get the job and if I made up an innocuous story, some vague but harmless medical reason, like flat feet, I was afraid he could easily check it out, and I wouldn't have a job either way. My first encounter with my suspect draft status, and eager as I was to start earning money and get a place of my own, I sat silent, confused. His friendly smile evaporated, his steely blue eyes boring in on me. I knew he knew and knew it was hopeless, so, without a word, I just got up and walked out of the place.

I found a job, however, with no questions asked, as a rate clerk at Waterman Steamship Company on Sansome Street down in the financial district and, while waiting for my first paycheck, began scouting around for a place of my own.

In the meantime, I stayed on with Tom and Paul at the Buchanan Street apartment, continuing to sleep on a narrow mattress on the floor—just like at Black Mountain—in the large front room. Tom and Paul shared the backroom, and since Tom worked nightwork and Paul worked during the day, they slept in shifts.

The rooms were spacious, ample and light enough for Tom and Paul to paint. There was a fireplace, and a large eat-in kitchen, which Tom enjoyed since he liked to cook and have people in for meals, and a black, blessedly unnosy landlord on the first floor.

Duncan was a frequent visitor, and Tom and Paul and Robert and I would spend hours in our free time sitting around the kitchen table talking writing and painting and all the gossip and shindigs of the Black Mountain and North Beach worlds. The apartment was also a hangout for former Black Mountain people, those already there, and an instant meeting place for any newcomers. It was a busy cheerful place, and although Tom complained at times, in his quick, fussy way, that all the socializing was interfering with his painting, he liked, just as he had at Black Mountain, being hospitable and could always be depended on to whip up a meal at a moment's notice out of practically nothing. Company was like oxygen for Tom who didn't at all like being by himself for too long. He couldn't have even if he'd wanted to since all our friends, and new ones, felt welcome there, and comfortable, free to drop in at any time.

Robert developed a particular fondness for Tom who, like Paul, was from Fort Wayne, Indiana. Tom always had a radiant tan, his hair streaked blond from the sun. He introduced me to Baker's Beach near the Golden Gate Bridge, and we'd spend hours there on clear days, lying on the sand and drinking beer (only the soldiers from the Presidio, blue from the bitter cold waters, swam in the ocean there, to impress their girlfriends), much as we used to on the boulders at Snake River summer afternoons at Black Mountain.

Tom was a simple heart, his generosity and good-nature often taken advantage of. He could be quickly hurt, and as quick to forgive. His abstract paintings at the time had a dense and lyrical richness. Sometimes exasperated with his compulsive endless chatter and slow flat Midwest talk (to drown the silences of uncertainty, it seemed at times, as if his gentle, slightly walled eyes were asking, "Love me in spite of everything, in spite of all I know myself not to be"), you couldn't help but respond to his earthy warmth and humor. His personal qualities were like adhesive, they stuck to you. They stick with me still.

One evening, shortly after I'd begun my new job, the four of us had supper together at Buchanan Street on Tom's night off, and afterward Tom asked Paul and me if we wouldn't mind going out for the evening. He said he and Robert wanted to spend the evening together. We said sure. Paul wanted to go off on the prowl alone and I headed for the bars of North Beach.

Since I had to get up early in the morning for my job, one that involved endless figures dealing with ships' ladings and manifests, I came home around midnight, figuring enough time had elapsed, only to find the front room, where I slept, in darkness. (Paul was already asleep in the backroom with the huge sliding doors closed.) In the light from the streetlamp I could make out Robert and Tom lying on the spare mattress by the big windows. They were unaware of my presence. Robert's voice was low and husky, his movements surprisingly athletic.

I coughed.

Tom glanced over to the doorway, smiled and said, "Give us a little more time."

I was tired and wanted to get to bed. I also knew that it was my job to wake Paul in the morning, a job that was—in spite of two alarm clocks under a washtub and a clock radio with the alarm set at full volume—like trying to raise the Titanic singlehanded. I said okay, begrudgingly, and went downstairs and out in the streets again. I walked for an hour, stopped in at a little neighborhood Oak Hill bar for a beer, came back, let myself in through the kitchen and found the front room still in darkness. I was disheartened to hear groans of amour, even more intense, from the mattress by the windows, and the energetic attentions of Robert even more strenuous than when I'd first walked in.

I coughed again.

They stopped, lay still and peered through the pale light at me standing once more in the doorway.

"Tom, I've got to get to sleep. I've got to go to work early. It's after one."

"So late?" piped Robert.

I came into the room. "You've had how many hours? Four?" I started to unroll the other mattress and make up my bed. "I'm sorry. I'm tired. And getting Paul up in the morning's like a full day's work, you know."

I didn't say so, but I was edgy with the complexities of learning a new job, and looking for a place of my own in my spare time. I badly needed the privacy to start writing again.

Robert sighed and by his silence and walk as he went by me to go into the bathroom let me know he was teed off. I felt like a heel. But if I suggested they simply ignore me lying in my corner I knew, having heard the pitch and heave of Robert's lovemaking, that I wouldn't be able to ignore them, that sleep would be impossible.

Robert had a few quiet words with Tom while he dressed, saying he ought to get back to Potrero Hill, Jess would be worried. Then he left, without saying goodnight to me.

As I took off my clothes, Tom, grinning, apologized for keeping me from my bed. "The hours just flew!" he sang in mock soprano and, lifting his arms and flapping them like a bird, did a little awkward dance around the room.

I smiled at his spontaneous performance through sleep-heavy eyes as I sank down on the mattress.

"Good night," I said. "Everything's all right."

It really was.

In my little one-room apartment that I eventually found after much looking, at $38 per month on Sacramento Street, ground floor rear on the shady side of Nob Hill, surrounded by the most quiet and pleasant Chinese neighbors from whose flowering trees red blossoms blew in at my windows, in a house Don Allen, the publisher, said, joking, looked like "it was designed by Frank Lloyd Wright," now working at a demanding job in the bill of lading department at the steamship company by day and writing at night. In my furnished yellow room the first thing I did was set up my "unconscious" altar on a handsome old chest-of-drawers, just right for it: the two Jargon editions of the *Maximus* poems on the right,

Jung's *Essays on a Science of Mythology* (a gift from John Wieners, swiped from the bookstore he worked in) to the left; above the chest, on the wall, center, I hung the broadside printed by Nick Cernovich at Black Mountain of Duncan's "Song of the Borderguard"—talismans and sustenance. Then I turned out the lights, lay flat on the floor and listened.

One evening, Duncan, sitting in the green chair in my yellow room, described Samuel Beckett's writing as "feeding on its own entrails."

At Waterman Steamship Company I always eagerly volunteered to take bills of lading to the Customs House for permits and to be officially stamped, along the several blocks route to the bay stopping every few steps to snatch my ever-ready notebook from my hip pocket to lean against a wall and hastily scribble down my latest thoughts, ideas, for what I was feverishly at work on at night in my yellow room over on Nob Hill (a story, "The Desert," an essay, "The Use of the Unconscious in Writing," and a critique of Ginsberg's new poem *Howl*). Such brief times out of the busy office and away from the ever-watchful eye of my boss made me feel a thief of stolen moments, all my real loot riding on my hip.

John Wieners taking me to a little bar he'd discovered near Chinatown that had a lot of Billie Holiday records on the jukebox. He kept savagely swishing his cane to the side and rear as we walked along Grant Avenue. He said it was to protect himself from Chinese undercover detectives following him.

Who's to say they were not?

Big, blond Dana, John's lover back in Boston and briefly at Black Mountain College, newly arrived in San Francisco from Massachusetts. Now removed from the certainties of family, job and the Swampscott Volunteer Fire Department, worried even more at not getting a job right away. Wieners tense over this but ecstatic to have him there. Ann Simone, ex-Black Mountaineer also newly arrived, driving John, Dana, Robert, Tom and me around the city one night soon after Dana's arrival, all of us somehow crammed into Ann's ultra-long Morgan sportscar with the thick leather belt strapped around the hood, as we barhopped and showed Dana the sights, his stomach very skittish from the jitters. Duncan very sympathetic, suggesting we stop at a drug store on Powell and recommending some over-the-counter medication for worried Dana to go in and get to calm down his gut.

Things got better when Dana finally landed a job in the financial district, and with John working at a bookstore in Union Square (keeping us all supplied with "gifts" of needed texts he boosted from the shelves—often taking special orders, Jung a favorite), the two rented a comfortable three-room apartment already furnished in 1930s style furniture, just around the corner from me on Leavenworth.

Late one Saturday afternoon soon after they moved in, they invited Tom and me to see the place and have drinks. After a couple of stiff rounds—Dana, the perfect host, doing

29

the generous pourings and getting pretty jolly himself—we all got quite giddy. John had been trying on some articles of drag in their bedroom and experimenting to see what shade of lipstick went with what, popping into the parlor on occasion to do a runway turn. Then, giggling like kids, we were all trying on the lipstick, tipsily, clumsily smearing it across our mouths. Suddenly there was a rap at the door, and when Dana, rubbing wildly at his lips with a handkerchief and shushing us with a panic-stricken look, answered it, there stood the landlord, a middle-aged, sober-faced man, who peered in at our own suddenly sober but lipstick-smeared faces with an expression of flat-eyed bewilderment, muttering, once he found his voice, "I was just wondering if you were settling in all right—any problems. . . ." His voice trailed off, and Dana assured him there weren't any. The landlord, gazing with uncertain glance around at us again— I had ducked my head and unsuccessfully tried to cover my mouth but knew my hand was not big enough to conceal the wild and erratic streaks of cherry red—nodded curtly and withdrew. When Dana shut the door, all of us, except Dana, relieved, burst into hysterical laughter. Dana, ever the worry wart, expressed fear that the landlord might chuck him and John out as perverts, but John, after blotting his mouth with cold cream and streaking on another shade of crimson ("the 5 & 10" always had the best selection, John assured us) told Dana nothing would happen. Dana calmed down a bit, and after another drink, even began laughing along with the rest of us at the baffled expression on the landlord's face.

After liberal daubings of John's cold cream, we cleansed ourselves of the lipstick before heading out for the 70¢ four-course dinner at one of the numerous cheap Chinese joints on Grant Avenue, before our night in the bars and coffee houses of North Beach.

Robert cooking supper for Tom Field and me while I read them a story I'd just finished, "The Desert." Robert frying up the usual gray meat patties (they always seemed to taste like veal, bought because cheap and money scarce) in his warm, comfortable kitchen, the bottle of wine Tom and I brought on table. Robert pausing over the frying pan, spatula in hand on hip, listening, occasionally shrieking with pleasure at a line he particularly enjoyed, rolling his eyes and laughing with that shrill, strong laugh of his. Tom, his face pink with wine, that small pleased smile on his face as he listened, a benign monk. Duncan's excitement communicating to me as I read, so that I really got into reading out the dialogue the way I heard it in my head in the writing. At Capon's granny-and-the-cat-in-the-oven story, he shouted, "Burning the pussy!" and clapped his hands, relishing it, and the character Claudia, a declaration of female absence from center.

He liked the story so much he suggested I send it off to Don Allen at Grove Press in New York, who'd recently written to Robert asking for leads on writing for the upcoming San Francisco issue of *Evergreen Review*. So I did, and sold my first story, at a penny a word.

On a late Saturday night, Ebbe Borregaard, tall, bearded, handsome poet, ex-army reject, and in at the end of Black Mountain, whom I fell in love with when I first clapped eyes on him in The Place, Joanne Kyger, poet and Brentano's clerk in perpetual black leotard "Beat-chick" garb, myself and a couple others, on our way to Dante's Pool Hall (Mike's) after Vesuvio closed. Waiting at Broadway and Columbus for the light to change and when it did, starting across when Ebbe, a little ahead of us, gave the finger to two guys in a car that almost ran over him and someone else, who I can't recall now, standing next to him. The car pulled over, the two guys got out, turned out to be plainclothesmen in an unmarked car and arrested Ebbe for "lewd behavior," and the person beside him.

Joanne and I went down to the Hall of Justice to try to get Ebbe out but we couldn't and he spent the night in jail.

Closing hour at The Place one Saturday night and looking out the window saw several police cars pull up and about two dozen cops in crash helmets hop out and line up quickly and silently in a double row facing each other from the entrance to the bar and on down the sidewalk. As we left the bar, a pretty sizable group, we were forced to walk single file through the aisle of cops who peered at each of us with close and tight-lipped scrutiny. A couple of guys ahead of me were pulled out of the line and shoved over to the police cars where, spraddled over the hoods, they were searched and questioned. I kept my eyes front and my lip buttoned and got through all right.

Jack Spicer carried his head in a flat, scrunched way, like he was expecting a sudden blow from behind. He became a turtle to protect the membrane of his sensibilities. Then, he became a turtle in a bottle.

Spicer was always crusty and short with me. After a first attempt at friendship, I soon gave it up. His mockery and wisecracks were more than I could handle, or understand. For whatever reason, he had decided to cut me out, and sometimes, verbally, cut me up. One night at The Place when Spicer had been particularly nasty to me, I got up and left the bar, earlier than I usually did. I walked toward Nob Hill in a black rage, silently mouthing in my mind all the comebacks I should've made to him. I simply couldn't comprehend his meanness. I needed cigarettes and went into a drugstore for a pack, still raging at Spicer in my head. The druggist behind the counter, a middle-aged balding man, gave me a sharp nervous look. I wondered briefly what was the matter with him. As I asked him for the cigarettes, he reached below the counter with one arm and kept it there, getting the cigarettes behind him and giving me change from the register with his free hand, all the time keeping an apprehensive, watchful eye on me, and that one arm firmly beneath the counter.

It didn't occur to me til I was out on the street that my anger at Spicer must have shown clearly in my face, and that I must have looked ready for mayhem or murder or, at the very least, undoubtedly to the druggist, armed robbery.

Ebbe Borregaard stayed for a time with Spicer. They had a special kind of friendship which surprised and puzzled me since Jack seemed close to very few people. I didn't understand then his profound distrust. As for me, perhaps it was because I was, then, mainly a "prose writer" and that he only wanted to spend his time and had more in common with other, younger poets, like Ebbe and George Stanley and

Joanne Kyger and John Wieners. Perhaps it was my own friendship with Ebbe, a rocky, unsatisfying friendship at best. Ebbe, an eminently sane man who had deliberately wrecked an overhead crane he was operating in order to get out of the army during the Korean War, so that he crashed with it amid a crush and tangle of metal and cables, miraculously unhurt; who, as noted, was tall with shaggy dark blond curls and beard, handsomely Nordic, exuding an intact strength, quietly blunt and direct, was, outwardly, super-straight.

Despite Ebbe's telling me he'd once thrown a school chum down a flight of stairs breaking his legs, for making a pass at him, I was gaga over him (perhaps because of that), and persistent. I finally wore him down. Booze helped. Spicer must've known. Perhaps that brought the meanness out in Spicer that he saw me as a threat I in no way wanted to be. Spicer was so close-mouthed and short with me, I could never have asked him any of this. It made me uncomfortable with him, and sorry, too, because it didn't have to be that way.

Duncan treated Spicer with respect, something else I couldn't grasp at first, being the newcomer on the scene. Robert told me of their longtime friendship from Berkeley days, and you could see that Spicer was respectful and quietly affectionate toward Duncan. Due to my own negative experiences with Spicer I couldn't share with Duncan his enthusiasms regarding Jack and his work. They talked as equals and spoke with a quiet seriousness, like two old friends who have long settled their differences and made a kind of comfortable peace with each other. Duncan behaved with Jack the way he behaved with Jess: there were no shrill and regal putdowns, no hint of the overbearing ego, the papal-like pronouncements, as with others. And Spicer's understated regard and warmth for Duncan continually surprised me (perplexed me, too, wanting some of it myself). Spicer could be so sharp and savage, and not only to myself. Yet I liked him, and respected him, too; admired the fierce integrity of his life and his work. Perhaps he had needed to make certain severe boundaries simply in order to survive. It crabbed him, stiffened him. We each do what's necessary. Maybe it was that, not Ebbe, not Duncan's generous response to my own writing, that set Jack against me. Whereas I took his rebuffs personally, Robert understood and responded to the more deeply personal man. As he said often, Spicer was another friend and poet who "fed" him. And looking back, after my own long and numerous bouts with booze, I understand Spicer more clearly.

Blabbermouth Nights at The Place when, judged by the enthusiasm and applause of the bar audience on the wit and verbal persuasion of the contestant, a magnum of champagne went to the best bullshit artist. (No small feat given the raucous cynics and critics in the crowd, mostly writers, musicians and painters, who weren't shy with their boos and catcalls, a fact which kept me a firm spectator.)

I don't recall Duncan speaking (or if he had, it would have to be a night I missed, since that would've been memorable, and I can't imagine him not winning, hands down), or Jack either, but Spicer was one of the initiators of Blabbermouth Night. His presence was very much in evidence as a kind of director, getting the contestants organized and lined up to speak. I never saw Spicer so excited and actively and socially involved as during those weeknight talk marathons at The Place. Perched on a stool at the packed bar, smiling, looking as if he were enjoying himself (a rare thing for him), he cocked his head and listened in foxy amusement, tossing out encouraging words or hissing loudly along with the rest, at the rant and hilarious exaggerations as each contestant declaimed in loud voice and sweeping gestures from the balcony in the rear.

Jack also enjoyed bestowing the magnum of champagne on the victor in a brief ceremony, shy and laconic in praise, almost embarrassed by his unaccustomed display of pleasure.

Once when I was teasing Duncan about his "harem of women" (Madeline Gleason, Helen Adam, Ruth Witt-Diamant, and others—no less foresisters such as H.D. and Gertrude Stein), mostly poets who would get together with Robert to read their poems and discuss them, he, who could be quite funny and cutting about them at times, said, "Those women are important to me," and with such seriousness I knew they were.

Duncan showing me a photo in *Life* of some "garden club-type ladies" dancing exuberantly and abandonedly over beds of exquisite flowers. They were like ecstatic whooping cranes.

Robert was immensely amused and shrieked with laughter at the photo as he leaned over my shoulder. I was amused, too, but a little saddened. "Maybe that's all they have," I said, "their neat gardens."

"They're actually frightening," he said and began to laugh his piercing laugh again. "It's like they're not dancing but trampling on the flowers. They need to kill them." This time there was an edge of vicious recognition in his voice.

Perhaps it was Kali he saw, many-armed goddess I dreamed of before I knew her name, who in a fury punches us back into life and out of it and keeps things kicking.

She lived in him, too, and he knew her well.

Robert telling me that Helen Adam's mother on her deathbed, after devoting her life to family, now elegant and old, propped up on pillows, dressed in a filmy negligee à la Frederick's of Hollywood, reminiscent, in Robert's fondness for the bizarre, of Miss Haversham, said to him, "I only wanted to play the piano." And Robert repeated her last line again, loudly, his voice quivering in a sense of wonder, and anger, too, at a life misused.

Of course, there was Helen.

Duncan had a friend who lived in a spacious Japanese-style house high up on a slope in Mill Valley in Marin County across the bay from the city. Duncan had gotten his friend to invite "Our Gang"—most of us looking a bit scruffy and defensive in such unaccustomed elegant surroundings—plus Robert's "harem," for a Saturday afternoon luncheon party in honor of Denise Levertov who had given a reading at the Poetry Center that week.

The party took a walk in the woods after the buffet

lunch, and walking with Denise and Mitch Goodman (who was her husband then), they both told me how much they liked "The Desert" which had just come out in the "San Francisco Scene" issue of *Evergreen Review*, words I needed to hear since Norman Podhoretz had just reviewed that issue in *The New Republic*, and had particularly singled out my story for a tongue-lashing, accusing me, in effect, of "masking homosexuality in religious symbols." I don't know if I was more upset at his negative view of "The Desert" or for blowing my cover. This was the first review of my work anywhere and its nastiness threw me. Duncan was especially supportive, as was Don Allen, co-editor at that time with Barney Rosset of *Evergreen Review*. Don had written to me, ". . . Please don't be upset by that review of *ER* 2 in the *New Republic*. Podhoretz is young and not very bright, and he's a protege of the *Partisan Review* people. His attack is what we expect, and no doubt there'll be more of the same, though more honest, I hope. . . ."

A few, like Ebbe and Spicer (Spicer was also represented in the "San Francisco Scene" issue), were gleeful, perhaps in teasing jealousy. Negative though Podhoretz was, it was at least some attention paid, although I could've done without it.

Toward the end of the afternoon we were all lounging on the broad open-air deck overlooking the valley far below and drinking wine when Robert asked Helen Adam to read one of her new poems. With alacrity, with the most genial of grins splitting that fascinating scrawny face, twittering with quick jerky movements, she whipped her poem out of her pocketbook and hopped up on the railing. Precariously perched there on the edge, with the steep drop down the mountain directly behind her, she commenced to read with terrific animation and energy, "I Love My Love," with its quotation from Robert, "In the dark of the moon the hair rules." I don't think I heard a word of it, certainly only snatches, for at any moment I expected Helen, jiggling her skinny body and gesticulating merrily, her voice trilling with grim pleasure as she read the magnificently wacky tale of the hair bound lovers, to pitch over backwards into the ravine below. But Robert, a grin on his face almost equal to the stretch of Helen's, was bobbing his body to the beat of the line and rolling his shoulders in pleasure with the ballad. If he did see the danger of Helen's precipitous fall, he paid no mind to it. He was, with Helen, enjoying himself immensely.

I breathed a sigh of relief when the poem ended and Helen hopped back down on the deck. The applause on the terrace rang out over the still, hazy valley. Robert leapt up and embraced Helen, twins of the black and bitter root of mirth—those two certainly knew something, then and now.

Olson read at San Francisco Museum of Modern Art and talked on Whitehead's *Process and Reality* at the invitation of the Poetry Center, through Duncan's involvement with the Center. First time I'd seen Charles since Black Mountain. In full beard, "I feel protected," he said. Informal talk on "The Special View of History" and reading at Duncan's place on Potrero Hill later. Olson expansive at front of the room, jammed with young poets and writers mostly; Duncan seated at his right, holding his body in a quiet position of identification and defense, sharp-voiced and sure, against verbal attacks on Olson and his projective verse stance from Michael McClure and Philip Whalen, fledgling and testing their own voices. Myself squirming with protection but Olson, as usual, quite able to take care of himself.

Joe Dunn's Sundays at his and wife Carol's apartment on Clay Street, two ex-Black Mountaineers and Boston cronies of Wieners. A saucer was passed to buy a gallon of wine and poetry was read by Joanne Kyger, Jack Spicer, Ebbe Borregaard, John Wieners, Robert Duncan, Philip Lamantia, Richard Brautigan, George Stanley, Tom Field, Nemi Frost-Hansen, Harold Dull, etc.

Or, if the San Francisco 49ers' game was on television we gathered around Jack Spicer at the Spider's Web bar on Polk Street to watch it. Discussions of the game were as heated and intense as those of the poems.

The Tin Angel, The Beaded Bag, The Black Cat, The Place, The Handlebar, The Green Lantern, Dolly's Doll House, Vesuvio, Tosca, The Silver Dollar, The Oak Room, Mike's Pool Hall, Co-Existence Bagel Shop, The Old Excelsior and Spaghetti Factory, The Fallen Angel.

The young black-haired Frenchman named André with the milkiest skin, in stark contrast to his navy-blue serge, wide lapel business suit and tie. Over here to look over *la scène*, he said. Tom introduced us in Vesuvio one evening. Said André really wanted to "get laid." Tom being "helpful."

After swift appraisal of me, André murmured he had a room nearby on Columbus and invited me back. Big old high-windowed room. Big messy unmade bed. Right off, André unzipped my fly, took out my cock and, very business-like, like a Parisian *poule*, carefully examined it in the bright overhead light. Then he placed it flat in the palm of his hand; hefted it for weight, eyed it for length—it was rapidly beginning to lengthen with so much handling. Squinting at it again, evidently deciding he could handle it, he stripped naked, lay on his belly amidst the tangled sheets, spread his pallid, hairless legs and whispered almost drowsily, "*Entrez*," the gleam of his nether cheeks as milky-white as his upper ones.

I was most obliging.

The strapping blond in his marine uniform turned out to be a twenty-year-old farmboy from Iowa. "Stationed at The Presidio," he offered, after I'd met him on Leavenworth late one Saturday night on my way home following an evening of no luck in the gay bars, the last try at the Handlebar down on California Street. Said he'd been "lookin' for a woman." He'd had no luck, either. Asked if I lived in the neighborhood, and did I live alone. Questions as signals he was probing, curious, maybe ready to settle for a guy, maybe secretly gay, making me think of the old queer sayings: The bigger they are, the faster they turn over. And: This year's trade is next year's competition.

So I invited him back to my place, not without that ever-present underedge of worry: the most innocent-faced are often the most murderously homophobic. You never knew who you were picking up. Still, to snag a marine, The Real Man at that time, although not that unusual in wide-open Frisco, was still a plus. And he appeared so fresh-faced, a cute, beardless boy, really, the archetypal fantasy of horny farmboy in overalls. I could see the muscles straining his uniform.

As we walked along, he, too, was concerned. Asked me if I was "all right." I assured him I was, whatever that meant, but he gave me a sideways glance that said he wasn't so sure.

Once at my place, he wouldn't take off his clothes and insisted upon doing it *under* the covers, which made it hot and stuffy. He kept saying we should leave and I should go help him find a woman. He kept on asking me if I was "all right," and did I intend to rob him. I tried to reassure him, but he wouldn't be convinced. Kept interrupting my attempts to get down to business by asking the same questions. I could see he was drunker than I thought, or more neurotic, since he had a tough time keeping it up, and that it'd be a long, jaw-breaking night for me. "Y'aren't gonna rob me, are ya?" he asked once more, and then unaccountably, as if asking for it, showed me a tightly folded twenty dollar bill hidden inside his belt buckle, "So nobody'll find it. I'm keepin' that for the woman." Avuncular, being a few years older, I advised him not to go flashing it around.

By this time he did have his neatly creased pea-green trousers down, but it was so sweaty under the covers and close, I could hardly breathe. And he kept asking me if I was OK. Then he muttered slyly, like he was offering me a big favor, "I know a lotta guys in my barracks go for this—You gimme your number, I'll give it to them."

Tempting as this offer was, as well as scaring the bejesus out of me, by then whatever erotic keenness I'd had for him evaporated, attractive though he'd been in my tipsiness out on the street.

By now I was pretty much sobered up, and seeing he was so fearful and distracted and that nothing was going to happen, I told him to pull up his pants and I'd go with him to help him find a woman.

"You're a good guy, and I'll really tell my buddies about you."

We went back out on the street, the overhead swirling fog off the Pacific a relief to my blanket-chafed and over-heated cheeks. After pointing him toward one of the B-girl bars down on Powell, the Yankee Doodle, I managed to duck him, praying he'd get laid and that if he didn't praying even harder he'd been too drunk to remember how to get back to Sacramento Street.

So much for A Few Good Men, I thought wearily, trudging back up Nob Hill.

A party at Duncan's, Robert leaning on a bookcase across the room; me dressed in my rate-clerk's suit and tie standing near the windows talking with someone. Robert, after several glasses of wine, announcing in a loud voice that "Undoubtedly some people are meant to be only clerks," and looking directly at me. The room getting quiet and people following his gaze. I couldn't meet his eyes, or speak, turned away and, because I hadn't been able to meet his lips, understood the slur.

Duncan several times told me of his friendship with the son of a wealthy family who had made their fortune in hot-water heaters. He seemed pleased to know this rich man, and his male lover, who lived a quiet, unflagrant life in comfortable surroundings somewhere over in Marin County. Robert on occasion had been invited to their luxurious house, or so it seemed from Robert's description. It was the glamor of wealth that excited Robert, its possibilities. He wasn't enamored of the rich, stuck on them, in the same way that F. Scott Fitzgerald was. Duncan had a sharp eye for the hypocrisy and apathy, the complacent coarsening that often accompanies wealth; the coarsening and narrowing that's different from that of the poor, the neglect and hunger (in all the appetites) that shrinks the expansion of possibilities.

As for me, I was fascinated by any gay who was wealthy (Ginsberg has described them as "elitist queens") because, mistakenly, I saw money as protection. A wealthy gay, as with any rich person, was untouchable, couldn't be caught by the law or, especially in my gay eyes, by the police who acted as hired enforcement agents of the oppressive anti-sodomy laws; in some measure, guilt-induced laws, on their return from the Wild West to the East, of our sodomite frontier forefathers, turned legislators. It was part of my twisted thinking at that time (although not completely twisted, the rich do have privileges in court the poor do not enjoy) that money, and the more the better, gave one the space to be free; that is, to be left alone. I didn't understand where the true wealth lay (in my own pockets), but I saw clearly from all the evidence around me that cash and paper wealth was where the power was, the power to be who and what you were, that enabled you to do as you had to do, in comfort and safety. (Now I know enough to always keep myself a little hungry: keeping the appetite sharp keeps the senses sharp, keeps curiosity and pleasure lean and active.)

For Duncan it was the additional glamor that money could provide, an extension of it: the farflung and exotic travel—". . . some monstrosity of history, some Venice. . . ."— the magnificent houses, the pretty dinners, the company of lovely and expensive men and women. (In describing his friend he said, "He has those sort of sleek good looks that only old money can buy.") But mainly it was the idea of money that excited Robert, excited his imagination, not the desire for it in abundance, or the acquisition of it. He knew very well the source of his own wealth, and drew on that. It's everywhere lavished in his poems.

But to me it would have meant safety, and a "respect" I desperately needed, courted and being courted by my own rich friends, in Philadelphia mostly, my lesbian friend in particular, who continued to write to me from Locust Street, pretending, at all costs, to be one of them, and at what cost. Fallacious, but there it was. And there I was, out-straighting the "straights" (no wonder Robert, in my writing, before we met, mistook me), careful not to offend, socially; maintaining constant vigilance regarding my slightest bodily movement or gesture, or tone of voice in public. When I got home from my job at the steamship company, after I'd locked the door and was finally alone, only then would the day-long tension in my face begin to ease, tension that was like neuralgia. Robert had no truck with this acute self-consciousness grounded, as mine was, in misapprehension and fear. He was, bravely, what he was, kowtowed to no one except when confronted with correspondent qualities in, say, a younger poet like Michael McClure or Richard Duerden. Then a lovely shyness entered his manner and voice, and a curious humbling respect, not abjectly but in recognition. Beauty, especially in a male poet, quieted him, seemed to throw him back again to a central need: to be fed through the handsome glamor and affectionate regard of such youths. It was what Whitman himself needed to nurture him. Their exterior qualities mirrored Robert's own inward ones. It brought him down, in a pleasant way; made him less harsh, less dominant and grasping, less talky. It focused the streams of his energy, more than Whitman, solitary and tormented, could. I marveled at his ability to find the sustaining affections he needed, in women as well.

Much of his nervous concern about his comings and goings seemed domestic drama in Robert's own head, a play of stealth common to any close relationship to safeguard and maintain the genuine center of his welfare and well-being: Jess and the familiar, protective abundance of the home on Potrero Hill, the sanctuary which kept his vision of love anchored and constant. As for the rest, they were laughy waystations of affectionate and intimate respite, no less important for that.

One day, when we were alone in his apartment and Robert had been telling me about his amorous experiences as a young gay, he brought out and showed me, rather shyly, photos of himself in his teens and early twenties. I was surprised to see the beautiful young man Robert had been. In an entry in her diary at Woodstock in 1939 Anaïs Nin wrote: "Robert Duncan—a strikingly beautiful boy, who looked about seventeen, with regular features, abundant hair, a faunish expression and a slight deviation in one eye, which made him seem to be looking always beyond and around you—read one of his poems."[4]

When I looked up from the photos to compliment him, the words died in my mouth. There was a hesitant smile on his lips, and with that curious asymmetrical angle of his eyes, he appeared to have one fond eye on the photos and the other, watchful, on my own eyes as my focus of vision turned from the snapshots of the Robert who was, to gaze at the Duncan now before me. The scrutiny of that eye on me had a timorous yet defiant look. I got confused, in the shadow of a youth on paper and the actual flesh of his presence now no more than several inches from my face. I tried to back down but his eye was close on me. "You were beautiful, Robert," I finally stammered. "And you're beautiful now, in a different way."

And it was true. But those who are beautiful, even when they begin to lose their beauty, still, out of the old habit of receiving compliments and attention for their loveliness, demand it still. Although Robert knew he was no longer the comely youth in the photographs, the expectations of admiration, so long assumed as a right and taken for granted, were still very much a part of him. Tribute must still be paid.

Part of my occasional discomfort with Robert—and our misunderstandings often I think hung on this—was that I could only respond to the Robert before me, love him in my own way, not the paper shadows of what he once was, the ephebe image of the slender and graceful young poet he still carried vividly within him. Perhaps this, in part, is what William Carlos Williams also meant by "the burden of loveliness."

There was also in the fearful but sharp eye glancing down at me, a silent, poignant expression that seemed to say, "You see me as I am now but this is what I was once." I sensed that Robert often felt he appeared to others, especially those whom he loved and whom he wished to love him, as a fattish, somewhat ridiculous figure who was shameless, lost all pride, when confronted with the impact of love, and its necessities. In my own greenness and incomprehension, I felt sorry for him at such times; the worst, and most arrogant thing I know now, you can feel for a person. At that moment, in the quietness of the front room of his apartment, I wanted to put my arms around him, to somehow comfort him for what he had lost and seemed to miss so dearly, but I couldn't. I cared for him too much in another way, as he was, to perpetuate the fantasy. And I paid for it.

He took the photos from my hands. "I'm a good ten years older than you," he said (Robert was then 36, I was 24). "You don't understand it now, but you will, when you get to be my age, and the younger writers are coming up."

In a blurred way I understood his words, what this meant, too, to him, as aging poet, words that have stayed with me and are now more sharply comprehensible as I move through the middle years. Its years give experience youth can only know in large, inchoate feelings, the winnowing to see what shape the day takes, all each of us are given. Nothing's taken away where something isn't given back again. I suspect Robert knows that, too; knew it even then.

The notorious bar down by the ferry at the foot of Market Street on the Embarcadero. Robert told me it was a hangout for sailors and rough trade that you could get anyone and anything you wanted there. So one Saturday night, my curiosity overcoming my apprehension, I went to check it out. The shabby bar upstairs, with cheap shots of whiskey, was noisily crowded with sailors and stevedores—many of them in the navy-blue sock hats and leather jackets and jeans that Jack Spicer wore—and working stiffs and Embarcadero winos. Robert had said the main action was downstairs in the cellar where the toilets were. After a couple of shots to give me the guts, I started down the wide, slate-worn stairs that made a turn into a huge fluorescent-lit room below, so that I could see—and be seen from—the whole area from the stairs, where I paused, the scene below giving me pause.

The room, with a cloud of blue smoke hovering near the nicotine-dark, tin-embossed ceiling, was also packed with men, but men who, while dressed like the guys upstairs, all looked queer to me. I could smell the toilets off through an entry to the left. In sharp contrast to the lively camaraderie in the bar upstairs, what was peculiar here was the total silence. What was also eerie and frightening was that as I descended the stairs all eyes lifted up to me, a sea of white faces—even San Francisco's tacit segregation was here—with eyes curious and calculating, measuring me in swift, appraising glances. Despite the booze, it unnerved me so, I stopped dead where I was half way down, my hand clutching the railing. The packed, hungry faces, the tart, pissy smell of the place, the acrid cloud of dense smoke, made me feel I was descending into a kind of hell. I turned carefully, and then fled back up the steps and out into the night.

I walked the length of the Embarcadero, trying to shake the vision of the place, to get the smell of it out of my nostrils, and out of my memory the fixed staring eyes of those men that had burned into my mind's eye.

One night passing by the alley between City Lights Bookshop and the Vesuvio Bar on Columbus Avenue, I saw half a dozen young men standing up on the front and back seats of an open convertible jammed in that narrow space, their bodies swaying silently back and forth, going at each other with broken beer bottles.

None of the passersby seemed to take notice or, if they did, walked quickly on. Unable to watch any longer, shaken, I went into the Vesuvio, sat by myself at the bar and ordered a drink. I got to thinking of Robert, and myself, and my other gay friends, and what that had to do with the guys I'd just seen midway up the dark alley, slashing at each other with jagged pieces of glass. They seemed a "type"—"Sunsetters" we called them, young men who would come into North Beach, usually on a Saturday night, beered up and looking for a kind of sex and action not found, or at least not as readily permitted, in their own neighborhoods. They came mostly from the Sunset District, a middle- and working-class area of San Francisco. I had had my own brief and frightening encounters with small gangs of them who had on several occasions stopped me in the street and asked me if I knew where they could get a "blow job," or "Hey, man, you look queer—How 'bout it? Right here on the spot." The young guy who said this to me one night on Grant Avenue was with such a gang. I tried to walk around them but they became threatening and I broke away; they grabbed out at me, and I ran as fast as I could down the block to The Place. I got lost in the crowd at the bar but, looking out the window, I saw the same guys milling around outside and peeping in for a couple of minutes. They didn't come inside, probably because the looks of the customers and the bar itself were a threat to them, an affront however tempting, being like nothing that was familiar to them, as yet, on their own turf. Such incidents were such a fairly common occurrence on the streets of North Beach, it didn't strike me to mention it to my friends at the bar.

Robert had known such men, young and not-so-young, white, usually; youths encountered in the street or at a bar, in a park, incidents he told me on occasion of his own youthful days as a gay male growing up in San Francisco and Oakland and New York City. One story in particular was about his being beaten brutally in a California park by a man who had made sexual overtures and Robert refused.

I had humiliated myself before them, too, mistaking their violence for strength, their often superb physicality and prowess for something other than it was, that kind of virility advertised everywhere in America as top prime, as the very best, and all that a man can be. I believed it, as I expect Robert at one time did, too. He had known also, as I had, in that most vulnerable position, after the adored one,

the chance stranger become familiar and exotic, the be-
loved, has spent himself, suddenly delivering the swift chop
to the neck or a blow to the head, pockets quickly rifled of
wallet, loose change; wristwatch snatched from the wrist;
rings yanked from the fingers (I never wear rings anymore);
another punch or kick in parting; the kneeling figure now
watching through surprised eyes (although not really so un-
surprised) as the man who had only a few moments before
shimmered before the eyes as a vessel, a containment of holy
flesh communion, now struts off with a sneer and a hitch of
the shoulders into the night.

Even as I had watched the young men stab at each other
with broken bottles in the alleyway, another, detached, part of
me, saw the lithe and rhythmically coordinated movement of
their bodies, vital, handsome faces, some gashed and bloody.
As I sat at the Vesuvio bar I wondered about that mute and
brutal fury that was everywhere like a male sickness and had
no sense or meaning in it. Is this what being male was? Was
this the natural order, the original instructions?

If I mistook random strangers for vessels of possible
love, and confirmation, it was because the shape was still
there, the substance of flesh, but they themselves were emp-
ty, as if a light had gone out in them and they lived in a half
world of poisonous attitudes, sealing off women, their own
within and those around them, unable to love them, or even
other men. There was no tenderness in them. They could
only then be truly Men, locked in their maleness, their agita-
tion, in violent acts, a battling within and without, both in
an unconscious need to escape the bind, and to strike out,
sexually and in physical harm.

Robert had served his own bitter apprenticeship with such men. The moments of fear I sometimes saw standing behind his suddenly startled eyes in the presence of them were eyes still amazed with a past I was myself then living through. It was not for nothing he sought the company of gentler, genuinely stronger men and women . . . of a Michael McClure, a Helen Adam, a Tom Field, a Denise Levertov, a Jess Collins, a Robert Creeley, or Charles Olson—whose strengths were grounded in acts of the imagination, the singular and spiritually muscular. Jack Spicer, too. Maybe Spicer had also learned that particular ugliness, "the recognition of disgust," as Duncan has said of Spicer, as mentor, and curb of his own excesses. Perhaps what Jack saw in me was another self, callow and vulnerable, without shell, as he had once been. Perhaps his ill-tempered crustiness with me was wisdom of experience—scars of accretion that formed, crab-like, his own protection—that knew that I must go through it all, and alone, to secrete and spin out of myself, against harm, against spiritual flab, defense and a protected space to come out the other side.

With the wider spread of drugs into North Beach by 1957, narcs were everywhere, especially in The Place and Vesuvio, dressed as one of the crowd in motorcycle gear or as Beat-type poets, right down to the jeans, black turtlenecks, even berets, and very friendly. You never knew who you were talking to. Among the hip avant-garde, everyone was on his guard.

Gay males had a double lookout not only for nosy narcs trying to pump them, often in more ways than one, but for the usual undercover cops in the Vice Squad, who were also everywhere. (It was the handful of queer bikers that confused everyone, in their burly black leather jackets and chaps studded with intricate rivet designs and clusters of faux gem-encrusted miniature wrenches riding on their hips, combined tools and costume jewelry worn for emergencies and fashion.)

With so many narcs swarming around, you never knew who you were buying from. So it was no wonder Eric Weinberger, slight, full bearded, another Black Mountaineer, was even more jumpy than he usually was, when several of us, including Ebbe, decided to chip in for some pot after Vesuvio closed one Saturday night, and Eric was picked to be the buyer from one of the inconspicuous dealers that were always hanging around outside the bars after hours.

Another major reason for concern was that pot possession could get you a stiff sentence in the slammer.

The rest of us watched from across the alley in front of Vesuvio while Eric, looking like a ghostly Jesus Christ, made the nickel bag deal in a shadowy doorway next to the City Lights Bookshop (where in honor of the recent banning of Allen Ginsberg's *Howl* by U. S. Customs, co-owner Lawrence Ferlinghetti had put on a full window display of banned books throughout history, starting with the *Bible* on through Joyce's *Ulysses*). When it was done and the dealer slipped off quickly around Broadway, Eric stepped out of the doorway, now the ordeal was over appearing even more grave and ashen than usual, and we took off for one of the guys' ground floor apartment in an old clapboard Victorian on Webster Street.

Once there, paranoia was rife, with Eric's perpetually sad eyes especially furtive, everybody on edge not only with anticipation of a high but fear of a bust as well, the latter not an uncommon occurrence in then-police state San Francisco, with the guy whose apartment it was insisting that nothing happen til he made sure every single window shade in the place was pulled down so tight that not even a crack of visibility for anyone peeping in was possible. The tenant even checked outside his front door two or three times to see if anyone was lurking out in the street before deciding it was safe, then firmly bolted the door after him. Just as we all settled down in a circle on the floor, and the first fat joint was expertly rolled by Eric (an old Bull Durham hand roller from Black Mountain days), lit and passed from hand to hand, the first toke shared, there was a sudden sharp rap on the door. Everyone froze. Was the dealer a narc and had we been followed? The guy whose place it was sprang up with a stricken look, snuffed out the joint, then at Eric's urgently whispered instructions, yanked open a window and frantically waved out the smoke, then hid the nickel bag outside the sill and slammed down the sill before creeping over to carefully unlock the door a crack and peep out.

All of us let out a big laugh when he opened it and we saw it was someone from Vesuvio who was in on the deal but had been detained and who had hurried over quick as he could so as not to be too late to get in a few tokes.

I had smoked pot in New York City with the guy I got a crush on in August 1956 during my vacation visit back to Black Mountain, the one who thought he was the reincarnation of Holden Caulfield, but that night's cannabis was the sweetest I'd ever known, and ever would know, a wonderful, honeyed high, that made everything truly right in myself, truly right in the cosmos. I sat at the feet of Ebbe, whose long frame was stretched at ease as he reclined on his side on the lumpy sofa and who was also feeling no pain. He had taken a guitar down from the wall and was idly plucking at it, softly humming some ballad, gazing from time to time my way as he played.

All the fears of narcs and Vice Squad undercover agents, of Jack Spicer, of my ambivalences toward Duncan, of the pressures of a new job and a new life in a new city, all the uncertainties of what it was I needed to be about, especially in my writing, momentarily vanished, as I gazed back at Ebbe, listening to his sweet guitar and the even sweeter sound of his voice as he sang.

The youth named Ahmed from the Middle East who worked in a gym down in Polk Gulch—"I love to watch the movement of the men's bodies." Met him in Vesuvio one night. Lean, exotic, dark-eyed beauty of an Arab with crisp black wavy hair. Took a shine to me and we ended the evening in my yellow room at the rear of 1430 Sacramento. Said he wanted someday to return to the Middle East and marry, but confessed to a "taste for buggery," and would I? I would. Body like a dancer, long thin limbs fanned out on the bed, insisting it must be belly down, not seeing my face, each movement a precise ritual, sacramental in its formality, a careful dance he carefully instructed me in, impatient when I made a mistake and did not please him, like a soft-spoken but stern choreographer of the erotic.

I was a bit put off, confused by his need to see to everything for his own pleasure, that he could not look into my face during this sensuous dance he stepped out in his own head. We made love once or twice more after that first night—or rather I followed his meticulous lead but finally grew weary of his erotically fussy perfectionism, sweet as the squeeze of that dark, silken-haired cleft was.

I began to avoid him at Vesuvio, and when he would ask me what was wrong, avoided those black, heavily-lashed, penetrating eyes as best I could. Late one night, leaving the Vesuvio and walking home down deserted Broadway, I sensed someone slip up behind me, felt a quick punch between my shoulder blades. Whipping around with an astonished cry, I saw to my surprise it was Ahmed, his eyes murderous slits, his thin lips twisted in a snarl as he growled out at me through clenched teeth, "If this had been a knife I would have slit you open—Next time this fist will be a knife—In my country that's what we do to those who betray."

And turning without another word, he began walking rapidly in the opposite direction.

My heart was beating wildly. I watched his dark thin figure depart, his muscularly lean shoulders held high. It took a few moments before I could catch my breath, then I too turned and continued walking quickly in the direction I'd started out in, still feeling the thud of his fist in my back, thinking, What if it had been a knife? I began to trot, then broke into a run, racing as fast as I could down Broadway, past the now closed Basque restaurants and the jazz joints, looking frantically over my shoulder every now and then, and didn't stop til I neared the foot of Nob Hill.

I stayed away from North Beach for several weeks, terrified of Ahmed leaping out at me from some night-time alleyway, dagger in hand. I refused to answer my doorbell either, which during that time rang insistently and often, certain it must be he. When I went out, I carefully checked both ways up and down Sacramento before stepping into the street. Finally, I heard someone casually mention, "You remember that guy Ahmed worked in the gym? Heard he decided to go back where he came from."

To say that I was enormously relieved would be to put it lightly.

It was Wieners who introduced me to bennies. After an evening of bar hopping in North Beach, an all-night delirium of bennie popping washed down with booze for a bunch of us crowded around the kitchen table in Tom and Paul's apartment on Buchanan Street. John with a sly grin and slow care removing the white Benzedrine pills from his pocket and lining them up reverentially on the oak table top for all to see, like communion hosts. Pointing with a smile of revelation as in a hushed, hieratic voice the quartered segments of each pill became in his eyes, and ours, "the cross of Saint Francis," that mystical connection underscored when he told us, his eyes again widening in revelation, that the St. Francis pharmacy across from the hotel of the same name was where he got his legal and illegal scrips for bennies filled, mostly 500 at a time. He'd been converted to them some time before and now wanted to convert the rest of us, "Especially you, Michael," he breathed softly, looking pointedly at me. "This is mostly for you because I know you'll get it the most." Then handing me the stark white pill between thumb and forefinger, that ecstatic smile still stretching his flushed cheeks, holding it before me like a priest extending a holy wafer, I instinctively opened my mouth and John reverently placed it on my outstretched tongue—two old altar boys, two old blue-collar Catholics to the core. (Duncan once jealously complained that Olson favored Tom, John and me more than him because we, like Olson, had been born Catholic and Duncan wasn't.) I washed it down with the cheap wine we were drinking—"This is my body, this is my blood"—an instant believer, while the others grinned, John's grin broader than anyone's.

A babbling brilliance around the table all night, or so it seemed. I'd never before felt such freedom of racing tongue and mind, a soaring clarity. I could not shut up. My conversion was complete. I truly felt a powerful laughy connection to all those at the table, truly flying with silver-tongued angels, especially with John who offered me "communion" several more times during the small hours of the morning. Several had already left but I scarcely noticed. I knew I had to get up early for work tomorrow, but I didn't care. At 8 a.m., still speeding after ten or more hours of it, I called the steamship company on Tom's phone, knowing my ever-punctual, early arriving boss would be there by then. When he answered, I told him I was ill and wouldn't be in that day—the first day of work I'd missed. He must've heard the high in my voice and asked if everything was OK. I assured him it was and hung up as quickly as I could.

It went on til two in the afternoon, John and I walking home in a sun as blinding to us as the whiteness of the bennies, famished for sugar and devouring anything sweet on the way, pastries and ice cream in Blum's on Polk Street. It took me hours before I came down enough to fall into a fitful sleep and days before I was able to resume my steady routine of work and writing.

But in spite of that, I knew I was hooked, especially upon discovering that after a night of drinking, a bennie or two took the edge off a sodden drunk, clarified and sharpened, made for a higher high without the staggering or the alcohol down.

I had to get my hands on a steady supply. John directed me to a doctor on Powell Street and instructed me to tell him I was "somewhat depressed and needed a lift." Without examination or question, the doctor automatically wrote me a prescription for 500 dexedrine tablets, which I immediately had filled at that same drug store John used.

They weren't the stark pure white of John's bennies, but bright orange, heart-shaped and smaller, warmer, more inviting, I thought (like the ones I used to buy from time to time to help me get through my grueling farm and kitchen work at Black Mountain, when I could afford them, at 50¢ a pop from the fat student who used them to control her weight, but didn't mind doing a little business on the side). I carried them, like grains of gold, in my pockets whenever I hit the North Beach bars, which was often enough, and particularly on the weekends when I would prowl the hills of San Francisco from night into morning, saucer-eyed on booze and dexies, desperately believing whatever I was looking for would be just over the next hill, and then the next and the next, never certain what it was I was searching for, some man, I thought, some impossible lover, and in wilder flights, some center of it all, some *Secret of the Golden Flower* (that Jung text lately also placed prominently on my altar in my yellow room); thinking of Duncan, who seemed to have that secret; stopping in all-night coffee joints to reinforce the high with strong black coffee, feeding the jukebox, listening, if Billie Holiday wasn't available, only to Johnny Mathis (who got his start singing a few years earlier at the drag bar Finoccio's in North Beach), my racing mind abuzz in hungry, isolate splendor.

Early one Sunday morning, still roaming at 4 a.m., I came across an electrical fire in a blown manhole on Geary Street, a great roar and crackling of a huge pure-white ball of icy fire that lit up the whole block, so bright it was as painful to look at as the sun itself. Alone for a few minutes before the police and utility repair crew arrived, I stared at that blinding, noisy luminescence anyway, vast bennie of the sun in the cold white fire of my amphetamine-charged brain, in the cold white crackling of my short-circuiting nerves, like gaping into a fierce inferno of empty, noisy light much like my own.

It took me several more years to kick the habit, that, along with a barbiturate addiction I developed to bring me down so I could sleep. Getting off the booze took a while longer. John became finally a speed freak, showing up several years later in New York, weighing about 90 pounds, long greasy stringy hair, long sharp finger- and toenails (so gone he walked about barefoot in dead of winter, wearing only a ragged short-sleeved shirt and thin cotton pants). Speed freaks were considered even by other addicts the lowest of the low.

In the early '60s, now living in a rat-infested boathouse, my Bowery on the Hudson 25 miles north of New York City, John one day wrote me about a troubled young ex-con poet friend of his who wanted desperately to meet me because he felt a powerful connection to my work, and believed I could "save" him in some way. I was dubious but my curiosity overwhelming my reluctance, we met and talked for hours at John's shabby apartment on the Lower East Side, the ex-con poet a small, pale, soft-spoken guy, the two of us finally crashing in John's bed while John, as always, speeding, paced about the cramped floor space muttering to himself and scribbling all night. John wrote me a few weeks later to tell me the young poet had committed suicide. I nagged at myself for months after, wondering if there was something I could have done. At that point in my life, there wasn't even anything I could for for myself. "Lucky stiff," I cynically concluded, rapidly reaching bottom myself.

After he moved out of Spicer's place, Ebbe reading Shelley to me the first night in his new apartment.

Kneeling before Ebbe, my arms resting on his thighs, thighs covered with dark honey-colored hair, hair like sleek animal fur, as he sits lordly erect in my green chair on the shady side of Nob Hill, peering down at me through the thick tangle of his eyebrows, me whispering, insistently, seductively, taking hostage, "All that you need is here in this room, all you need is me, here, the world shut up, shut out; just the two of us together, here in this room. . . .You don't need anything else. . . ."

He says nothing, just keeps staring down at me with

his impassive, fiercely handsome face, the heat of him still tingling in my gut, that heat of him rising up in my throat, putting desperate words in my mouth.

Walking with Duncan down Market Street, after we'd just seen the first of Jacques Cousteau's under-ocean movies. "I could be happy living only at the bottom of the sea, like some sea-creature. It looked so still there, so silent," he said, eyeing, in a glancing, insouciant way, the sailors, most of them young and lean and gangly, rolling bright-eyed high along the sidewalk, looking for action, the surprise of unexpected pleasure. Robert himself (as Olson also once noted) occasionally wall-eyed in moments of extreme intensity, his peripheral vision open-seeing, learned at the borders of seeing, of language, crossing and recrossing to the heart of, to further reaches, distances. Myself, then so brainwashed with internalized homophobia I was embarrassed for him, but mainly frightened at his openness, his flirtatious eyes. My own eyes watching out for police, the plainclothesman, not knowing then it's not only the cops in the street but the cops in the head you have to watch out for.

In 1958, shortly after I left San Francisco for New York I received a letter from Joanne Kyger which sums up in large measure that frantic, exhilarating and energetic time:

The poetry was very exciting yesterday with George Stanley, obviously worried because he had not written anything for at least a month being hideously bitchy about a poem of Harold Dull's which caused Robert Duncan to become very emotional and go from defending Harold's poem to defending his own poetry and thank god Jack Spicer came to his rescue so it was the old folk against the young folk (Stanley, Ebbe, Brautigan). I was pretty high on wine so I don't remember the exact exchange of conversation except that Pip [John Wieners] said that he had never felt so close to Duncan before. Robert had been pushed to the point in which he forgot or discarded his usual rhetoric about writing and made very personal statements about what he was doing. Perhaps someone else can tell you exactly his words when they write. Robert read part eight on the Structure of Rhyme [sic].

Enclosed is a new poem.

Pip came by Friday night with an assorted collection of Kids[5] and after taking a bennie stayed until five in the morning working on a translation of Apollinaire which he read yesterday.

I have stayed away from North Beach for a whole week and Nemi [Frost-Hansen] has painted murals on my hall wall including a lovely panel of a purple hound peeing against a tall tree. I must remember never to move.

Three

There are many things that I could relate but perhaps it's only one story I have to tell out of so many, of Robert or myself or others, in that time in San Francisco. And it's this:

One Saturday night I'd been at the Blackhawk, a jazz club near Polk Street, listening to Miles Davis. Kenneth Patchen and others used to read their poems there to jazz. I was walking home alone, back to my apartment on Sacramento two blocks up from Polk. It was, for whatever reason—fatigue, or just the hassle of it, or maybe it was that standing at the far corner of the Blackhawk bar Miles Davis seemed to be aiming his horn directly at me, and that made my night—whatever, it was just one of those rare nights I didn't feel like going home with anybody.

Polk Gulch, as it was called then, and may be even now, was the main drag for heavy cruising, the boundary line between heavily gay populated Pacific Heights and Nob Hill. At that late hour there was the usual number of men walking slowly, eyeing each other, or standing looking out from darkened shop doorways. But I wasn't interested that night, just kept on walking and minding my own business, Davis' trumpet still tootling in my head, a curious strangled horn of remorse.

As I was about to turn up Sacramento, several policemen came up behind me. One, with a round face and mustache, said to me in a quick, low voice, "You know that guy?" pointing to a young man walking several paces ahead of me. I told him no, looked at him and the two other cops with him, surprised where they could've come from so suddenly. The cop with the mustache said, "Yes you do. I saw you talking to him. You were trying to pick him up." I stared at him in disbelief and said I wasn't. He said, "Get in the wagon." Before I could say a word, the other two policemen grabbed me and fast-stepped me into a police van parked at the curb about a half a block back, while the round-faced cop hurried up the street and stopped another young man.

As I climbed into the wagon it was already pretty crowded with other men, mostly young like myself, sitting quietly, heads bowed, on the side benches facing each other. The doors were slammed shut and through the rear windows I could see other youths being approached by the cop with the mustache and, after a few brief words, hustled off by his cohorts to several other wagons parked at intervals along the street. It was all done so quickly and efficiently, the police advancing silently up the block from the rear in their dragnet, none of the men on the street suspected until it was too late.

In spite of my confusion and growing numbness (it had finally happened!), I looked around at the faces of the other youths. They sat slumped and mute, staring straight ahead with blank eyes or down at the floor. I wanted to say something to the man next to me but he avoided my eyes. I too kept silent, no longer trying to see the eyes of the others, and looked again out the rear windows. Two policemen leapt up on the back runningboard, the doors were locked and the van began to move at a high speed. There were no sirens.

Through the glass I could see the faces of the two policemen. They were the ones who had put me in the van. They were hanging on the back, guarding the doors as we sped away. One was blond and fair and had a decent, innocent face. It wore the look of the impassive cop, revealing nothing. I wondered if this was a learned thing—I've seen it so often—a part of police training. You see that kind of face everywhere. It's a face I've always wanted to have and started to practice trying to acquire in my adolescence, as a kind of protection, but never could: a flat stoic face that betrayed nothing of what went on behind it. Not the black or Native American face but an American male face: white, expressionless, and safe, where only the mouth moves a little.

I had always thought such a face concealed much strength and mastery, even mystery. I know now what it conceals.

We were taken first to a local precinct where we were packed into several small cells. There were about thirty of us. One by one we were brought out of the cells and searched. I was writing a great deal at that time—I had over several months since my arrival in San Francisco written, besides "The Desert," an essay, "The Use of the Unconscious in Writing," and a critique of Ginsberg's *Howl*—and always carried a small notebook with me to get down any ideas or lines of dialogue or bits of description. The policeman who searched me found it in my inside pocket and casually flicked through it.

"What's this?"

I told him it was stuff I'd written.

"Yeah? But what's this mean?" and he pointed to a sentence I don't recall exactly what it was now—but it referred to some thing specifically gay; rare for me, my struggle and guilt with my gayness were so overwhelming I took care to leave out of my notebooks any overt reference to it; it was also this moment that I feared, getting arrested.

"Something I wrote," I said.

"I see that," he said with dry contempt.

"I want it back." I held out my hand.

He looked at me for the first time and it seemed all the hatred he could muster was focused in his eyes.

"They'll take it away from you anyway when you get where you're going."

My heart raced as he slapped the notebook down on my open palm.

"Where am I going?"

"You'll see. Bring in the next one," he said to the policeman behind me.

(I've only recently begun to feel safe carrying a notebook I've been writing in with me into the streets; not always, and it depends where I'm going, even now.)

As I walked down the dimly lit corridor to the cell with the young policeman, he touched my arm and said quietly, first looking over his shoulder to make sure there were no other policemen in earshot, "Don't worry. It'll be all right." It was small comfort then, but it was at least something. It was said in spontaneous simple kindness and although I wasn't able to respond to it when given, I never forgot it.

Back in the cell, two policemen were taking each man's name and address. When they got to me I gave them the information they wanted in a voice tense with fury and fear. The cop taking down the information glanced up and fixed me with eyes drained of anything resembling human eyes: frozen and locked without a glint of understanding. He peered steadily at me as if he was observing some loathsome subhuman thing.

"I'll remember you," he said. His eyes snapped down coolly and he stepped off to the next man. (And I did see him several months later at Market and Powell one evening, a popular rendezvous spot for picking up street tricks and hustlers, a silk scarf tossed casually about his throat, his topcoat draped loosely over his shoulders, hands clasped seductively on hips, so obviously a stereotype queen on the make, plainclothes vice cop stuck out all over him. I wanted to laugh, go up to him and say in a loud voice, "Good evening, detective. How's tricks?" but thought better of it and crossed over Market to the other side.)

My perceptions were probably distorted by my own concerns in those hours, but I don't recall speaking to another gay prisoner that whole time. I don't remember any of the gay prisoners speaking to another. After an hour or so, we were taken out to the wagons again and transported to the Hall of Justice where we were packed into the drunk tanks.

The one I was put in was already half-filled with Saturday night drunks. At one point a woman was brought into the station her arms held firmly by two cops. I watched through the bars. She was drunk and hollering she wanted to fuck every cop in the place. The cops were joking and kidding with her. She seemed known there. The cops winked at each other as they took her away to the women's tanks where I could hear several prostitutes shouting obscenities and screaming that they wanted bail right away because this was their busy night on the streets.

After a while the gay prisoners were taken upstairs in small groups where we were booked, fingerprinted and mugshots taken. The photographer was bitching because this unexpected dragnet meant he had to work overtime. I was thinking of my picture in the police and government files for years to come, available.

I was charged with vagrancy, as were the others. You could be charged with that in the City of San Francisco at that time if you didn't have $1,000 in your pockets. It didn't matter. That wasn't the real charge, and we all knew it.

(Such gay dragnets were not uncommon in San Francisco: The police either needed to fill their monthly arrest quotas or it was election time, with city hall politicians campaign-promising to "clean up the city," and what more vulnerable group was there to "clean up" than the queers? And, as in the early days of Hitler's Germany when homosexuals were rounded up in Berlin and sent to prisons and finally to concentration camps, who would stand up for faggots? Who would care?)

Downstairs we were each permitted one telephone call. I didn't know who to contact or where to call for help. In New York a few years earlier Ben Weber, the composer, told me that if I ever got into trouble as a gay with the police to call the last name under "Z" in the Manhattan directory. He said it was the name of a lawyer who defended gays in police entrapment and bar-raiding cases. But this was San Francisco and I knew no lawyer's name to call. I didn't try to reach Duncan (who didn't have a telephone anyway) or John Wieners or Tom Field. What I needed was bail and I knew none of my friends had any money.

The cop by the phone gave me the number of a bail-bondsman, one of the many in storefront offices I'd passed many times across the street from the Hall of Justice. I called and within two hours he appeared, apologizing because it was Saturday night and he was busy (like the prostitutes had been), a short plump man in a scruffy topcoat. Bail was set at $200 and I paid $20 cash fee, which I fortunately had with me, to the bailbondsman (no small amount for me in those days). Another hour or so in the tank while paperwork was being finished and I was let go, told to appear in court at 11 a.m. on Monday.

When I got out on the street it was dawn. I felt drained of energy. The worst was the uncertainty in knowing that I had to appear in court, to stand up in front of strangers and be judged by strangers. I worried if my name and address would appear in the *Chronicle* or the *Examiner,* common journalistic practice in such arrests in those days (both papers read by practically everyone at work), and if I would lose my job.

I wanted to tell Duncan and Wieners and Tom but I didn't know how. And what good would it do? I'd been unlucky. We'd joked about such things happening, blunt humor with an hysterical underedge of terror. I'd gotten caught. All the fears that I faced as a gay male every day of my life were not new to me, but being arrested and spending some hours in jail were. As I walked back to my place on Sacramento I kept thinking of D. H. Lawrence's phrase (given in a somewhat different context) in *The Plumed Serpent*, "Don't get caught." I had always that unconscious instinct of guardedness, of self-preservation. It hadn't always worked but I'd never gotten locked up. It's curious (and not without its humorous side) that I should get arrested not "in the act" but as any other citizen simply going home to go to bed.

And trudging up Nob Hill, heavy with fatigue, the blue light of morning fanning over the city, bed was all I could think of.

I worked in the Alaska-Commercial Building on Sansome Street. On Monday morning I only told my boss, a squat, muscular Swede who was mostly pretty decent with me, that I had to leave early for lunch. He didn't like it and I didn't explain, but he said it was okay. (There were several gay males working in the office, and we knew each other—one, in fact, worked in the bill of lading department with me—but the extent of what was shared together was limited, in bitterly flippant and cynical internalized self-loathing, to sex and bar experiences; I shared none of what happened to me over the weekend with any of them, unwilling to risk a possible attack of the biting mockery and jokes so many of us survived on, keeping the ugly reality at arm's length.) I walked the few blocks to the Hall of Justice. I didn't know if I was coming back. The main thing was to get it over with, either way.

George Stanley was at that time working as a clerk-typist in the Police Department in the Hall. Just a few weeks before my arrest I'd had lunch with George and, after, walked back with him to his job. We were both feeling in a giddy mood (that other San Francisco, the open city, could do that, often). As we stood joking for a few minutes at the entrance to the building with policemen and detectives hurrying in and out or standing talking in groups close by, I made a remark about the *Howl* trial, which was then in progress, upstairs in a court room in that very Hall of Justice, something about how absurd the whole censorship root of it was. The papers were filled with news of the trial and the main talk in the North Beach bars centered on it. It was particularly on my mind since I'd just finished writing a critique of *Howl* for *The Black Mountain Review*. I'd barely gotten the words out of my mouth when instantly George's expression changed. He became suddenly serious, his face went in a split second from laughter to caution and apprehension. He quickly put a finger to his lips in warning and rolled his eyes from side to side in the direction of the policemen and detectives around us. It threw me for a moment, and yet I instantly understood. *Howl*, among other much needed revelations, celebrated gaiety, the first since Whitman. George, open among friends, was in the closet working as a civilian clerk for the police department. My expansive mood shriveled and again I saw that same look in George's eyes that I'd seen in the eyes of the men I'd later be arrested with: shame and anguish, an overpowering sense of helplessness. It was like a light went out in me, and in George, an extinguishing I'd known so many times.

So many small deaths.

That morning as I walked into the Hall of Justice I was afraid George might see me in the building, that I would have to explain. It also had to do, because he knew me, with putting George and his job in jeopardy. But so much of this had to do with an old habit, with working things out on my own, not trusting or relying on others. Variant, and realizing this from an early age, I'd had to develop an ingrained habit of self-reliance and of trusting my own eyes. There had been nothing or no one else to rely on. Certainly not the family where the terrors within for a queer child were as frightening as the terrors without. No gay liberation group, either, to turn to for support and information then. The Mattachine Society had been founded by Harry Hay and a tiny group of gay men and, later, lesbians in Los Angeles in 1950; I'd heard rumors of their existence but knew nothing of their work.[6] The Stonewall Rebellion marking the spirit of '69 didn't occur until over a decade later.

It also had to do with shame and anger that so many of us shared, a vicious dishing on each other, a gay version of doing the dozens, that only kept us more isolated and hostile toward each other, unable to speak sure and supportive feelings; even Duncan to a certain degree was hamstrung by this insidiousness of traditional attitudes that had become an unquestioned, official reality. I hadn't yet been able to come to terms with this shame and anger, to take pride in what I was, to let the rest of it go, make truce with it; no longer pretend to be what was unnatural for me. And that's come through time, and a protected sense of space, through myself and others. Knowing, too, that the Great Spirit doesn't exclude me.

The courtroom was packed. I supposed it was always so on a Monday after "The Great American Weekend." I took a seat in the back and looked around at the faces of the men closest to me, but, perhaps because of the bright daylight pouring in through the windows, I didn't recognize anyone I'd been locked up with Saturday night.

I was dressed in tie and suit. I tried to appear as "respectable" as possible, speaking to no one, keeping my eyes front, not to get too close to that dangerous identity, here in this place where my freedom would be decided. Hating this feeling and not understanding why, then.

The drunken woman taken into the tanks on Saturday night was one of the first brought up before the judge. She had spent the weekend in jail and was accompanied by a matron. The judge told her that she'd appeared before him many times now on drunk and disorderly conduct charges. She hung her head, nodding it slowly as he spoke. She was blond, perhaps in her 30s, attractive. She looked neater and trimmer than on Saturday night certainly. You could tell she'd taken care, as I had, to look as presentable as she could.

The judge asked her if she had anything to say. She began to speak, at first hesitantly, then her words becoming more and more impassioned as she said how sorry she was, tried to explain that she'd gotten drunk again by mistake, didn't know how it had happened, she hadn't had a drink for so long—and then, well, she didn't know why it was. She began to flatter the judge, thanked him for past leniencies. Her hands darted with quick pleading movements, her voice breaking and vulnerable with just the right pitch of little-girl weakness and helplessness. The judge watched her with his head aslant, amused and pleased. He'd undoubtedly seen it before. It was a good act. She performed it well. So well that she earned her release, the judge letting her off with a warning that next time she'd spend a month in jail.

"Thank you, your honor, thank you," she cried in a loud, grateful voice over and over, tears running down her cheeks. I burned with shame and commiseration for her. But I knew she was only doing what she had to do, what was expected of her.

After several other briefly handled cases on the court calendar, the names of the men arrested with me in Saturday night's dragnet were called. The assistant district attorney seated to the right of the judge addressed him with a brief summary of the time and place of each arrest as each man was called, the majority of charges being for vagrancy and loitering. Most of the men said they wanted to speak further with a lawyer. Some insisted on a jury trial; one man in particular in a firm assertive voice—a new sound to me, that a gay had that right. I secretly admired his courage. But the mere thought of a jury trial appalled me; I knew what kind of justice to expect there.

When the assistant district attorney called my name I stood up. I could feel all eyes on me although I'm sure they were not. The assistant district attorney read off that I'd been caught standing in a dark doorway with another youth, that we were talking in a way that suggested solicitation, which the arresting officer corroborated. I wanted to shout out, He's lying! But I, who all my life had been unused to speaking out in self-defense, kept still, that inner voice of protection saying, Keep quiet and maybe you'll get off, get away.

I stood as erect as I could as I listened to the distortion because no matter what uncertainties churned inside me—and my heart was slamming heavily—I was convinced of my innocence, in my actions of that Saturday night "soliciting" or not. My anger at having to be placed in such a position of judgment, in such a place, and before such men, only stiffened me with contempt and an affirmation of a different sense of pride, also new to me.

The judge asked me how I pleaded. I said, "Not guilty," as loud and firm as I could. The judge leaned over and conferred with the assistant district attorney for several moments. It seemed to take forever, their confidential whispering.

I had no words then for what I was, and am (except the pejorative)—that didn't come til years later. Then, forced to be other than I was, I only knew I was being tried in a court by the same people in positions of authority who had told me all my life what I could and could not do with my feelings, my love, my sensuality, and my life. I hadn't the awareness that I got years later from other women and men that finally turned all that personal negative energy around. Surrounded as I was by gay males in the court room, there was no one to stand up with me, nor anyone to stand up with each of them. We were isolated from each other by guilt and shame and the profoundly inculcated belief that we had no natural right to existence, all that accepted and contagious determination that was embodied in the police, the judge, the assistant district attorney, the very law of the court itself as microcosm of the entrenched ignorance of centuries of the broader society at large.

Finally the judge spoke. "We haven't got enough evidence here. Charges dismissed."

I said nothing. I walked out of the courtroom quickly. Up until the time my name was called I was the only one who had pleaded not guilty. The weight of the past 48 hours lifted but the effects of that experience were to stay with me for many years. I had almost gotten caught. After that, I became more cautious in my habits, more closed. I began, in earnest, to learn a perfect frozen face.[7]

I was hungry. I had a quick sandwich and coffee and hurried back to work.

I kept silent for several days, told no one. It would have been easier for me if I'd been able to loosen up. That part of me I had had to keep in a tightly sealed closet. San Francisco had been an opening up, in my writing and my life. It was this part that kept getting shut. I didn't know how to respond or reach out. A few days later I tried to tell John Wieners but it got all broken in the telling. I could sense his outrage, his sympathy, but there was no open ground any of us could share, no precedents for solidarity. Except the writing, as a focus and center, a place. John had been beginning to speak up, plain, in those strong early poems, "A Poem for the Old Man," "A Poem for Cocksuckers." Duncan, too; the thread there in many of his poems, and even much earlier, extraordinary for its time, his bold and astute essay "The Homosexual in Society," in the August 1944 issue of *Politics*. I still spoke through a gauze mask, keeping my nose clean. Mistaken health. Mistaking these early voices of Duncan and Wieners and Ginsberg, the handful of others, with alarm, with a tighter hitch in the surgical mask. And around the neck, a chokening of the "priestly" collar, "The Desert" metaphor of that shrinkage.

Robert was shrewder, had, through his own past experience, learned the importance of a secret I stumbled to learn, and yearned to know. Duncan knew the horrors and fragmentation of street-life for a gay male and took care that his friendship with Jess and their home together remained intact and central in a deep instinctual sense of containment in one whose sensual energies and attentions streamed everywhere. It literally kept him off the streets I haunted. The time and energy I spent in the magnetic pull of chance and surprise in the flesh of numerous men (the chance and surprise of that numbers game becoming more and more mechanical and empty), Duncan was able to concentrate in the poem. The foundation was his love for Jess, in the "one who was also many." Robert sought others to love, more often only as an occasional feedback, to freshen and vitalize, peripheral to the focus Jess was. It wasn't the addictive, far-wandering search of the streets and the bars where I mistakenly thought what I needed was, not knowing that I carried it inside me, as Duncan did, that what I needed wasn't outside to find, but right under my nose, in the house of my own skin. I needed to nurture it there within a shielded structure, as Duncan did. I didn't know that simple secret so many others took for granted. There was so little, and still is, for the gay to pattern that necessary structure on. The lesbian or gay male in the family is, more often than not, as I was, an outcast, an alien. As in my own family I had no firm sense of knowing how I belonged, or how to. Quite literally, I didn't know where I stood; there seemed no right place for me. I did everything double for whatever scraps of affection or praise from my mother and, especially, my father. My needs were of a different order from my brothers and sister, essentially because of variance, and the fact of that variance being, whenever acknowledged, or suspected, misunderstood and never permitted. "I've been cast out and I will be avenged." The need for a place to be was so terrific I went to any length to find it. So perhaps it was that I hitchhiked, to New York, to Black Mountain, to San Francisco, to find a habitat to receive that. But I ended up looking for it in places where it wasn't. I searched outwardly for what Duncan had carefully and wisely made for himself, his own necessary enclave to work and live in.

I watched to learn his secret, yet couldn't get to it, or get it down. Duncan gave to me, and to others, a sense of what liberation could really mean, not as sexual licentiousness, as cock addiction and the numbers game: he taught me there's no freedom without walls ("The walls! We've got to have them!" Olson once exclaimed). But it's important the walls are of your own making (not those imposed from without by others) to exist and work in openly and comfortably in expansive affection and vitality; in the distance of impersonal affection that respects the singularity of the beloved, and one's own, the space to move and make in: *home*, that most powerful word, in all that it means. Otherwise the swarm rushes in, assaults and fractures, and in the fragmentation energy spills and is wasted. What I sometimes saw in Duncan's domestic confines was actually the footing, the grounding, that broadened his capabilities. My own "freedom" in the streets and bars and beds of San Francisco was the real confinement, a prison of strictures in which stuck repetitions denied illumination. It kept me in the dark.

Running, scared of never finding it, looking in all the wrong eyes and places, I spilled my energy and concentration everywhere.

Duncan knew better.

Forced to the fringes, I took to the mountains in my head, became a guerrilla, became self-reliant (like so many others), built stamina and slyness, made forays on the dead center, with act, with words, on a land, a globe, halved in dominance from which, split, non-cohered, all that's done then emanates from negative energies.

Got caught by the deathpack. Managed to escape. Got caught again. Again escaped.

So many forced to take to the mountains; Black Mountain an enclave, learning, guerrilla-like, in Swannanoa sanctuary beyond the mainstream which had become an arroyo, if only that were known, and many more are knowing it.

"Nature has first claim." I will be intimate with nature. Put my ear to it, listen. A weed is more important than the hydrogen bomb. My hand, coursing with blood, more important. No mind can make a weed, or this hand. Shoving everything up into the mind in pure white hubris, nature denies us. Its punishment is terrible. It puts out your light and makes a kind of shadowland where nothing's perceived with clarity or seen for what it is; where all is a flat sameness, of no value, not equal, not intra-nourished, inter-constructed, but leveled, mediocre. Denying, it can only eviscerate. Eat.

Duncan knows "the delightful play of existence." He, too, learning in the silent hills to look in and out. At all of us strung up on the cross, crucifixion of flesh 2,000 years. Time to come down off that cross, claim the body again. Love it, honor it, the containment of ground and firmament gods and goddesses. Deferred pleasure is death. All propaganda deferring joy and celebration is death-dealing. Even the meanest weed sparkles in the sun; dances in the wind. You also stream the body with light again, your eyes will be lighting the darkness around.

Robert Duncan's poems are his eyes. Ours, too. They light the ground and air.

How long it's taken me to get here, even to be able to write this down at all. At that time, I simply couldn't.

As I've said before, this was also the time when Allen Ginsberg's poem *Howl* was on trial, being tried by Judge Clayton Horn in those very weeks in that very courtroom, the same judge I was brought before that Monday morning almost twenty years ago.

Far worse things have happened to others, I know, with far worse results. But it doesn't matter. Like alcohol or other drugs, it doesn't matter what or how much you take, it's what it does to you. What this did was take years away from me. But I've learned now one's life can begin anytime one chooses, out of need and occasion, and then begin again. All is all right, beyond our cherished ignorances, those human, and tenuous though brutal, impositions and is as it's meant to be, and if it took me a long way around to go a short distance (to paraphrase Melville), it was worth it.

This, on the face of it, seems a great deal about me. But it's also very much about Robert Duncan not only because he's a great poet who also happens to be gay, but because to be gay in San Francisco at that time was to know not only what I knew and faced daily, but what he, and all of us, knew as well. My story is his story, and theirs; we shared the same experience, all the gay women and men shared the same. The details of our stories differ but at root they were each the same: that in some deep and vital part of us we were hobbled and misshapen by the sickness of homophobia that permeates America from top to bottom. And still does, as it's done 4,000 years and more in the Western world, cripples and impoverishes all it infects of whatever sensual affection.

I'm a survivor, too, and Robert Duncan; we are all survivors; and proof, in my words, as he is in his, that I saw that I didn't die, almost, but didn't, and was strengthened, given a resilience and new passages. I see a hummingbird tethered to a grubby stake that has, of necessity, found other ways to fly, deflect to the world the magnificent iridescence of its wings, and the sounds the breath of its wings make. I hear that, see it, and know it in my own hummingbird heart when I read and hear the poems of Robert Duncan. He pollinates the gardens of the earth in his poems, the gardens that yearn to blossom secretly in the innermost primes of all of us.

Robert Duncan gives tongue to that, and speaks for all our unuttered hearts in celebration, is vibrant and living testament of it. This ruby breast of the Hummingbird Spirit is flying everywhere again.

South Nyack, New York
1976–1977

Endnotes

1. Essays on several plays of Shakespeare.

2. By Peggy Tolk Vaughn Watkins, first in Sausalito, then in San Francisco.

3. Ginsberg told me, on March 2, 1976, that he read "Howl" that night, one of three readings of the poem he gave in San Francisco at the time, shortly before leaving for Los Angeles, Mexico, and Tangiers. That particular reading was arranged by Ruth Witt-Diamant, head of the Poetry Center at San Francisco State, and was held at a school, according to Ginsberg, "about four or five blocks from The Place—I think it was called the Greenwich School." He also said he was "pretty certain that I'd been there in The Place that night after the reading with the rest of the crowd."

4. *The Diary of Anaïs Nin, Volume Three, 1939-1944,* edited by Gunther Stahlmann; Harcourt Bruce Jovanovich, New York, 1969.

5. Poets, painters, writers, friends of Joanne, whose nickname was "Miss Kids."

6. *Gay American History: Lesbian and Gay Men in the U.S.A.*, by Jonathan Katz; New York: Thomas Y. Crowell Co., 1976.

7. In this morning's *New York Times*—March 30, 1976—a headline on the front page tells us that six of the nine justices of the United States Supreme Court "DECLINE TO REMOVE CURB ON HOMOSEXUALS." And in a sub-headline: "High Court Says States May Jail Violators Even If They Are Consenting Adults." However, legal sanctions not needed for sensual disobedience.

SELECTED LETTERS
MICHAEL RUMAKER / ROBERT DUNCAN

edited by Ammiel Alcalay and Megan Paslawski

Michael Rumaker was the first in his family to graduate from high school, which made Black Mountain College an unlikely but necessary destination for him. After his family threw him out "for not going to church and for being queer," Rumaker happened to attend a lecture by the artist Ben Shahn at the Philadelphia Museum of Art. Shahn had taught at Black Mountain and was enthusiastic about it and his good friend Charles Olson, who was soon to become its Rector. Mary Reed, a friend of Rumaker's who taught painting in Philadelphia, was aware of the college: "Oh yes, Black Mountain, I hear it's a hotbed of communism and homosexuals." Such credentials convinced Rumaker to matriculate. These initial letters (one from Robert Creeley and an exchange between Rumaker and Robert Duncan), discuss Rumaker's final examination and graduation, which at Black Mountain required an external examiner instead of tests set by a student's teachers. The college chose Duncan to examine Rumaker.

Robert Creeley to Michael Rumaker, October 9, 1955

Dear Mike,

[...] I'm sorry not to have been here for your graduation—they tell me it was terrific, and I'm very happy it all went off ok. As to Robert D / he suddenly went all 'academic,' i.e., wanted to know if you'd read Henry James, and so forth, i.e., must have felt suddenly called upon to act as a 'scholar' or some damn thing. It wasn't at all that he felt any diminishment re that feeling he had for your writing, much more literally; but again, thought I guess he was called upon to deal with it all, i.e., graduation-wise, very much in this other 'character,' which is no more his than mine. The outcome is, no one has that kind of time; and as far as we are concerned, it does not affect anything. I.e., it would take too damn long, and is not the point to begin with—so to hell with it. But again, do let me emphasize this was Robert's sudden flair for academicism (apparently) you bumped into, we bumped into—not any lessening of his more relevant sense (opinion) that you make it, as a writer. Which is all anyone wanted to know, in the first place. Wow. [. . .]

Robert Duncan to Michael Rumaker, March 30, 1956
[*The major portion of this letter appears in the text of* Robert Duncan in San Francisco]

[. . .] It is a matter of some ten years between me and thee. And in another ten years when you start reading the "new" writers you will see it more sharply. Especially when that ten years is the difference between a depression and a warboom; between a world that was just beginning to know that there might be war and a world that will now never believe there might be peace.

Michael Rumaker to Robert Duncan, April 4, 1956

Dear Robert Duncan,

[. . .] I'm sorry if graduating me put you in a bad spot. I had great doubts towards the end as to the validity of it all. But at the time I had such great doubts about so many things. I don't think I can make much sense on the subject. Only to say that some redefinition of 'graduation' is needed as far as Black Mountain College is concerned. Certainly the education there isn't the job-preparing type that education now has mostly come to mean; nor is it culture, art, taught as a pastime or hobby, or worse, a come-uppance superiority. I think of "enclave" from [Norbert] Wiener and how much it seems to apply to the place, but only if you make it that, for yourself—granted desire and the intensity to outreach yourself, to change. And men there to give you clues, as they do. I went there wanting something. And found it. People say, oh you could've gone anywhere and managed it on your own hook. But the difference "anywhere" is no clues and, hence, no news; also the confusion of the practical as opposed to the possible unconfusing of the impractical—the latter being a luxury of education to be found only at Black Mountain. So that a graduate might be measured by how close he has arrived at his own enclave within the larger structural enclave of the college, how much he is involved in and committed to his work, its pleasures and reliefs—and I mean as assayed by his work accomplished, not by him as person/personality: everybody's got problems. This strikes me as the only possible standard for what graduation might mean at the college. At least in my own case I sensed it without putting it into words, as I'm trying to do here and perhaps badly. It's just that I feel anything would be too confining and irrelevant. One can't think in other graduatory terms because, as Black Mountain is set up, they just wouldn't apply. What does anyone go there for, except in hopes of putting an end to confusion, of actually getting a foothold in themselves and their work, because other institutions fail. I know, many go there and dawdle, waste themselves, because they have neither the stamina nor the desire, finally, to make the vital change. I don't see how Black Mountain can be anything more than for just a few—but this can't be foreseen and because of that no rules can be made to exclude anyone—because <u>possibility</u> is so tremendous. One never knows. It takes a burning to fully utilize what Black Mountain has to offer. Otherwise one can mess around or shell up, exist effortlessly there, as nowhere else. The mountains are pretty. [. . .]

From the formality expected between student and examiner, the letters between Rumaker and Duncan soon become more familiar. Excited about Black Mountain Review *and on his way up to New York for some temporary work to make ends meet, Duncan writes Rumaker on May 12, 1956, saying that he would be sending five copies: "Use the extras to whatever good purpose you can to introduce the Review and try to solicit subscriptions. I want to get the list up to one hundred subscriptions by the time we have to worry about financing and publishing the next issue. When this semester ends in June I am going to trek up North again and maybe then can arrange to visit you. I have a job open typing in New York at a pretty good wage to keep things going between semesters (or through*

the summer if the summer session doesn't go thru)." Rumaker
promptly writes back on May 21st, busy "trying to boost cir-
culation," as he takes copies of Black Mountain Review *to all*
the bookstores in Philadelphia and is met, surprisingly, with
enthusiasm in shop after shop: "After lunch I went to Joseph
Fox's bookstore on Sansome St. and his place is very small and
in a basement and right away he started complaining that he
couldn't take on another quarterly because he just didn't have
the space, but when I whipped out the copy of the Review he
sat down, looked at it and melted." This engagement in lit-
erature and its distribution couldn't prevent his home town of
Philadelphia from feeling more and more oppressive, and the
idea of going to San Francisco took hold in Rumaker.

Michael Rumaker to Robert Duncan, September 19, 1956

Dear Robert,

I finally got your address from Mary F. [Fiore] I'm leaving
for San Francisco on October 15 or 16—probably hitchhike
as far west as I can; plane too damned expensive and you
don't see anything; train a drag, cost more than the plane,
figuring meals, wear and tear, etc. Anyway, I'm having my
stuff shipped air freight (trunk and typewriter) and want
to know if it will be all right to have it sent care of your
address. Friends advised me that they knew plenty of people
in Frisco but when it came to a showdown turns out they
only know them slightly or haven't seen them in years. You
see, I'd wanted a place to stay until I found a job and could
get a room or something of my own. So if you know some-
body who's willing to put up with me for awhile, I'd be very

grateful. If worse comes to worse I'll put up at the Y, but I'd rather not have to do that. Also, if you hear of any not too impossible jobs available, I'd appreciate it if you'd keep me in mind. Will you let me know what you think of all this as soon as possible?

Am getting very excited about going away from here. Have started my journal again (due, I think, to your enthusiasm), and a nutsy story, meandering and sick, just going on and stopping and braking, all the parts loosely connected, trying to see if I can write from the "I" since the invisible third person doesn't seem to want to work right now. But I'll get back to that. I really believe once I get out of here I'll be all right again. I'm not expecting anything great in San Francisco. If it's there, fine. If not, okay. But it's the change I need, 'the new scene', and it's that I know will stimulate and get me going again. Can't sleep here, can't work and everything gets more and more tangled. Impossible and stupid. [. . .] Hope to hear from you soon.

Love,

Mike

Robert Duncan to Michael Rumaker, October 5, 1956

Dear Mike / "As soon as possible"—and here it is two weeks at least since I received your letter. Yes, you can send your things care of me at this address [1137 De Haro]. Where we will find a place for you to stay is still up in the air. When I got your letter I phoned Tom Field who was looking for a place himself—but I haven't seen him since. If that worked out, it might be easiest for you but however it goes

I think I can find a corner of this city ready for you when you arrive.

I am just getting down to correspondence again—two days ago we were given a perfect little writing desk, almost classical for letters: so it is a pleasure to sit and write on and maybe on. Jess has finished building all the book-shelves and the books are somewhat distributed, and paintings are on the wall, and we are in debt for a handsome new Columbia phonograph model Kilosphere: it is like living.

News comes that Black Mountain has suspended operations (for the winter?)—Wes had me call him long distance to ask me if I could find out if there was any possibility of enrollment around here for one of BMC's G.I.s; and also to ask if he might find a theater out here. I wonder if there would be any chance of any of MEDEA's cast coming west?? I finished that first play, you know—for production there. Ann Simone is almost irreplaceable—Now, having completed the "Preface" for Letters, my task is to do some re-writing on the prolog for the play: and to submit it then to a theater group here. The Poetry Center plans for a theater failed to find funds.

We are looking forward to your arrival—

Love, Robert

Michael Rumaker to Robert Duncan, October 8, 1956

Dear Robert,

Along with your letter today was a second letter from Tom telling me that he has moved from Kearny to Buchanan St. Tom had written earlier saying that it would be all right for me to put up with Paul and himself and I was waiting to hear from you before telling you about this. So this will unburden you of having to think of a place for me to stay. I will ship my stuff to Tom's place and will, of course, go there when I arrive in San Francisco. I hope to be able to get a job soon and a place of my own, and from what Tom and others say, there seems to be quite a few jobs around. And it will be good to see you again and to meet Jess. I hope to leave here Monday, the 15th, hitchhiking. My route goes through New Mexico and I plan to stop off there and see if can find Creeley who, as I learned from Ian Robertson, is teaching in a small boys school outside Albuquerque. I wrote Robert a letter about this last night and I hope he answers with directions as to how to get where he is (tho he might not want to see anybody, and I can understand this). I met Ian and his wife at a Farewell Potty Ann Stokes gave for me Saturday night, and they both struck me as very fine people. I talked to them a great deal and they told me how they are doing your Letters and Creel's The Dress, and all about Joel's [Oppenheimer] book, etc. etc. Very exciting. He also said he would like to do a book of mine, "next year", which floored me. It was fine at first, I mean the idea of it, but the next morning I began to realize that I don't have much that would be printable and so I'm now feeling glum about it. I promised to send him some mss—Exit 3, Loie's Party, and so forth—but what I really hope is that I can do some good stories when I get situated on the coast, because here I've really run dry and as I was telling Creeley, what I have done here is all pretty neurotic, pretty sick—re; Digging—all abstract misery; and even the River lacks a total involvement, none of the joy or pleasure in the writing as in those earlier stories, and when these two conditions are absent it's a sure clue for me that a story isn't going anywhere. And I'm getting good and god-damned confused here, more than is good or necessary, so fuck it. People keep asking me <u>why</u> I am leaving Phila,—Now all I say is: fuck it. I've never met so many amateur psychologists as lately. I must look like a field day for them. I try to explain to them quite honestly and seriously WHY I am leaving Phila, but they never seem to understand or hear that—they keep popping up with these coined conclusions that I'm "ESCAPING" and "RUNNING AWAY", "WEAK, and not facing up to reality"—saying it owl-eyed and wise as tho they had thought up all these conclusions themselves last Tuesday. So now I just say fuck it and if they irritate me bad enough I make up fantastic neuroses, blocks, complexes, many of which they've never even dreamed of. Well, I don't want to get started on them. Some day I'm gonna write a story about them—a whole cocktail-partyful of them and turn on them, like a hose, the most fantastical bizarre creature I can manufacture.[. . .]

While Rumaker and Olson's shared interest in dreams and the unconscious has been more closely documented elsewhere, the following exchange of letters shows the intensity and enthusiasm with which Duncan greeted Rumaker's short but highly influential piece, "The Use of the Unconscious in Writing," which he eventually published in 1963 in The Moderns: An Anthology of New Writing in America, *edited by LeRoi Jones/Amiri Baraka.*

Robert Duncan to Michael Rumaker, June 5, 1957

Dear Mike /

Yr *Use of Unconscious* piece arrived today, and straight off I send my <u>From These Str[ ]</u>s, somewhat abashed [. . .] I've been at the idea of the proposition. Here you are working the definition and whetting (not wetting) my appetite—my mind must ready to take up this insistence to be after the what-it-is, yes, I might and would have, other things to say about the psychic-physical thing—and out of that the metaphor, simile, and symbol (but, especially these last are terms for—and remove from experience into pedagogy : do for me.

What I mean is that a horse is a [triangular drawing]. & also a ground of crystal hearing that drives the eagerness. Also a horse is like a dandylion [sic] = fluffy and field-blossoming. A horse is extinct and monstrous. Come to the horse who speaks without words. Etc. These demonstrations including said horse I saw and other I rode which was leaps of confidence. Any of these demonstrations are hopelessly (as [illeg] is by those other terms, iamb, trochee etc.) neutered general out of their particular insistence by grammatical definition.

But: just so—you carry me along <u>with you</u> in territories where if not driven by your essay I would pontificate : make my own empire.

A pleasure anyway to be reading where mind has been in action, to feel the drive of the sentence with that will

tripe = the indiscriminate = that which has not been discriminated.

there is the sense that a total intensity is possible—in which, well close [ ], yes, but not to weed value from valueless : but in discriminating value from value to FOCUS. There is no item in the universe that is not properly essential content & hence "to the self its contents"

unconscious <———————>unknown
of the self of the universe

There are things in this essay we may all be borrowing : "a thickening process, that gathers for charges"

re: symbol in greek συμβολή (verb συμβάλλομαι)
= meeting, joining : as in the flowing intogether of two rivers; or the jointure.

II. in hostile sense, an encounter, a battle   III. συμβολαιον a contract

IV. συμβολαί contributions made to a common meal,— the meal itself, a picnic

The verb (above). συμβολέω = to [ ] or fall in with a συμβόλαιον (your symbolism?) = a token, a symptom II. a contract, covenant also III. intercourse of men & women Plutarch Alexander 30

ideogram(two riversmeeting place
  offlowing in tojoint
symbol each other)(suture of the
  out(man ⟵—→ woman)skull)
of greek
a communiona battle

or

    pick-nicka contract

don't some of these remain in our language today of a contribution to a communal picnic. "This is a sign of my affection" "he sent a token" "I will sign the agreement."

But "sign" is more potent in meaning than symbol. It keeps the multifariousness of an event. "I saw signs that deer had passed this way." "The sign read—keep to the left" "This is the sign of an educated man"

It is because we are aware of a signature or the sign of an event that a rose is a symbol, a thing shared or in which a series of events share. The cross is a sign of the sun's journey—of the four directions defined by the sun's journey and then, later, of the wheel (or the wheel is de-signd to embody the journey) it is upon this : The cross-roads from which no soul could escape that Christ (the anointed is crossed)

    Some notes in partial appreciation
    Yrs
    Duncan

Michael Rumaker to Robert Duncan, undated/unsent

Dear Robert,

~~I don't know why you've haven't written. I guess you have reasons of your own. I send you these things not with the idea of your possibly printing them. I want you to see them.~~

And perhaps, if it strikes you, to tell me something. But I would like to hear from you, not necessarily on terms of one writer on another writer.

~~Enclosed~~ Here is The Desert. The thing is, that when the heat of doing it cools—that moving out of and, quite like, a going "back" into life—it seems then a mere-going-on-ness, that read-back flat, not as fresh and vivid as the first imagining. And it's the removal from the thing, the going out of it, away from. A recoil. As I think I told you I almost burned The Pipe—~~thinking, when finished that it was first, too fantastic to be believable and secondly, the words flat and stale. And it's just that I had done it and was thru with it and it was time to move on to something new. And now, I feel, with this.~~

But there is still the necessity of another looking at it afresh, with the distance of not having made the thing, the distance of the reader with whatever degree of involvement the writing demands.

I want to know if it hangs together. I want to know if it's 'all there'—as you once wrote me The Pipe was. How does the dialog strike the ear, the language? (I can't hear it anymore).

The "going-on-ness" I've been criticized for. But without that method of staying close to things, of "pushing the penny with your nose", as Olson says, I don't arrive. I don't apologize for that method because it's the only one, right now, with which I can operate and know that the writing's not false, that it's something close to the nature of myself, my own processes. For myself, at present, I see no other approach to story. Outside it, to try to get free of it, is casting about, a discomfort at not being there, where things can occur, lies, and not be false. That seems to be the limit, the method, which demands obedience. But within it are innumerable possibilities of change, of invention.

In The Desert Billy is now William, a much more formal, less shy and chaotic creature—at the threshold of seeking to discover the manhood of himself. The hard thing has been to say, to make articulate, what William must articulate: to get it out, however haphazard, wrong-sounding—that he is, as he says, "a mistaken man"—mistaken and makes mistakes, if only to get to, to find some clue to, himself. [. . .]

As William says: the hard-won innocence of manhood. Because the innocence of childhood is given, free. But because of that, easily lost. The innocence of manhood is an earned thing. Not so easily got, not got without struggle in, around, and for the self. That a man most often must get driven to the [illeg] ~~it with his own blood.~~ What it is once got, I don't know. I know only bits of it, ~~(in anger or in fear or in delight)~~, faint comings and goings in myself—the rest is a dream of it— William's, and the fierce struggle to attain it—that he is driven to the inhuman in order to find again what is human. We have lost so much of it, if not all, that what remains, remains in dreams, reminding. ~~me.~~ Which is why the unconscious. Which is why our desperation is a measure of how much we have lost of this thing: what it is to be a man, a woman. [. . .]

Implicit images, meanings, perhaps there from what the physical brings about—I think of it all after—the nonphysical intent that my need to obey the physical seems to make happen unconsciously—what you once wrote me—"a deeper, unconscious power operant."

For at the end, I see meanings that I didn't put there

consciously—and if not consciously they must stem from the unconscious. It seems that an intense preoccupation with the physical yields psychic responses. The meanings don't get there by accident. And I sense also operant an under-logic, not the conscious one, that brings about an interlocked structure of things within the story, without my willing it. That's its first intensity, and second, involvement and preoccupation with the physical that sets up the involitional force of the unconscious, its contents moving parallel with the known, the improvised-on conscious contents. A rhythm, as car gears meshing, each touching and causing the other to move, grabbing and gibing, to prompt and yield the substance and power of each—and absolute rhythm of movement, instantaneous, going.

That a story can be, obliquely, a map of the unconscious. Its terrain and peopling. The landscapes which draw you, actual or imagined, are the landscapes of the self. The unconscious nests the actual, the unknown one posits itself on the physical one, invisible [illegible], each moves, in the act of writing, concurrently, creates an open structure in which one is free to invent, bound neither strictly to the unconsciousness nor to consciousness, but an interchange of the powers of each in which the humdrum can occur as the psychic contents respond [as well as talk that] all is believable within the framework of the story since all is created between those two poles of force.

Rumaker, still fighting to find the security he needed to openly express his desires and intellectual truths, left San Francisco unexpectedly and suddenly. In New York, he danced at Amiri

Baraka's parties by night and by day wrote letters of unhappiness and despair to Joanne Kyger. In its immediate aftermath, the one sure accomplishment of his move back east was its establishment of the distance from which he could appreciate Duncan more. As he wrote in this undated response to the publication of Duncan's poetry in Measure, *"Robert, Your 'Propositions' in* Measure *is. . . . I can't find the word. I'm thrilled, and moved. You're the richest man in San Francisco."*

Michael Rumaker to Robert Duncan, May 28, 1958

Dear Robert,

[. . .]I met Robin Blaser Saturday afternoon. He was down for the weekend from Boston. Don Allen was with him. I met them at the Kline show at the Janis. I liked him very much. He had such a naïve frankness about him and he was immediately curious and warm. We had a whole afternoon and evening together. (The Kline show was really magnificent, the only disappointment is that the gallery is too damn small to get far enough away to take them all in, <u>and</u> the crowd—there was one particular beauty, all color, bright, raw and vigorous—no sense trying to describe it—I hope you will see it sometime; unfortunately, I've forgotten its name) After a few more galleries (one show of Frenchmen, including Dubuffet, who, in contrast to Kline, looking piddling), Allen, whose passion is bridges and Weehawken, N.J., took us up to the Geo. Washington Bridge entrance and we walked across to Jersey. A fine, clear day, NYC not as savage from across the Hudson, and we stopped off at several typical N.J. roadhouses for beers along the way and even got to ride in a cab with a bleachblond taxidriver who's collaborating with the local doctor to writer another "Peyton Place" on Weehawken, an ugly, industrial town hugging the foot of the cliffs and the huge plant of its chief industry—ALCOA—built smack around the town's only cemetary. Then, before getting on the ferry to get back to N.Y., we stopped in this ancient, sagging bar where seamen and truckdrivers and the local "quaints" hang out, including one of the town's policemen who Robin sat next to at the bar and he was drinking rum with orange bitters with a Coke chaser and had sweaty hair curling over his ears and hated the barmaid in a jocular, threatening sort of way—she, appeasing, with free drinks—and got along well with Robin telling him about all the local murders, rapes, and monstrosities with a kind of relish—"Are you a schoolteacher?"—complaining of the "New York bunch" who come over and raise hell in the town and give him a lot of trouble. He was actually touched, and pleased, that we had walked over the bridge to see the place and the view from the jersey side. One ear cocked to them, while with Donald I had a long quiet, really pleasant, talk about writing matters. It was a very good day and I felt in fine spirits and the ferry-ride back was wonderful and that evening we went to see "Les Enfants de Paradise" which I didn't like very much. It was terribly wrong, I <u>mean</u>, long! And Don and Robin couldn't understand why I didn't like it—I supposed I don't have the temperament for that sort of thing. Finally, caffe espresso and pastry at Bizarre. If I ever get to Boston I hope to see Robin again. And I'm hoping, some weekend, to make the trip up, especially to go on to Gloucester to see Charles [Olson], who's been very much in my dreams lately. Once as a healer, another time as a sort of "magician" with plucked eyebrows penciled back. We talked about you and both wondered about John—Robin hasn't heard from him either. It was amusing the picture he had of Joanne Kyger. He'd heard that John had "moved in with her" and he pictured her as a scheming, poisonously sophisticated harpie-type! So I tried to explain Kids to him, tho that's almost impossible, and he seemed a little relieved.

There isn't much that I can tell you about anyone since I don't go downtown very much. Haven't seen Basil or Martha [King] as yet, tho I did see Jerry [van de Wiele] and his wife at the Cedar St. one Saturday night a few weeks ago. They had just gotten in. Jerry was very eager, flushed, it seemed, from his Chicago successes, and ready to turn this old town on its ear. Mitch [Goodman] & Denise [Levertov] I saw just that once. It's all pretty distracting and I try to keep out of it as much as possible. I mean, it all seems to make me confused and I don't come out of it replenished in any way. [. . .]

Say hello to Jess.

Love to you,

Mike

In the fall of 1958, Rumaker entered the Rockland Psychiatric Center, whose name in Howl *represented one of the ways a repressive society had attempted to destroy the best minds of a generation. Rumaker's two-year stay is revealed in letters and journals. He later described this time to Don Allen as the start of better things for him, but in the meantime his survival depended on maintaining the connections, intellectual and personal, he had with other writers, artists, and queers.*

His letters to Duncan from this time are raw and document the depths to which Rumaker had to go to emerge again, freer, stronger, and more prepared for a world that mostly had not heeded Duncan's 1944 call for true human interrelations.

Michael Rumaker to Robert Duncan, September 26, 1959

Dear Robert,

It's very clear to me that my soul is a donkey, overwhelming inert and needing the right (the accurate) kick in the right place, the Master and foot of the spirit, to get me going again, moving off, I need a master.

I need his "sanctions"—oh, a child of God—to protect me, and my heart aches, I think of my father, I think he took it as a slap in the face, a humiliation, having a son 14 lbs. at 6 mos., a sick nuisance and growing up weak and effeminate. "you curl your hair," he sd.

He wouldn't have anything to do with me. Then enters the fantasy of the changeling which puts down the mother and the father as the child has been put down. 'They aren't a queen. They'll come to reclaim me.' The orphan, set apart, something "finer." The measure of the putting down in the intensity, the long hold, of the fantasy and the loathing, the apartness. The obverse of love.

"Milk," he sd.

"Sperm?"

"Mother's"

"What?"

"Love."

"Baloney," I sd.

I keep telling him it's too late, but he doesn't say anything, doesn't commit himself, take the risks, as he asks me to do, expose myself, be vulnerable, be left holding the bag.

No, it's not justifications—no more of that! Sanctions. What, the flesh and the blood needs justification? a crime against nature? against who, pls?

A crime against my donkey, listening to them, pushing this way and that, and themselves not knowing which way to go.

———

a wonderful warm full day and the boys sprawled side by side on the grass of the golf course (I found a brand new golf ball I bounced all day). And Dr. Stanley, The Director, taking down the names and bldgs. of male patients walking with female patients, and going to the Exchange and taking down names of male patients sitting having coffee with female patients.

"I want to smash everything. I want to smash these gray clerks of the soul. I want the day back. I am not a psychopath. I am not nuts."

I asked Dr. Walters why not let the patients have sex, so what? And he says, Lawsuits.

Money behind it.

(But "nature has first claim.")

Trying to look at it like a savage parting the grass, it's unbelievable that we hand the needs and desires of the flesh and blood into the jurisdiction of the police.

(Brooks Adams saying the origin of Protestantism

occurred when the merchants no longer wanted to pay for miracle but wanted to get it cheap—and finally for nothing.)

Sunday

I'm wondering if anyone'll come to visit me. If not, I'll go out for a walk and mail this.

Pls tell Joanne I hope everything goes well—she didn't answer my last letter

And say hello to Jess.

Love,

Mike

Tell John [Wieners] "Early Risers" <u>wonderful!</u>

Michael Rumaker to Robert Duncan, sometime in 1959

Wednesday

Dear Robert,

An androgynous young man has just brought me a liverwurst sandwich. There's no milk. The sandwich is dry and spicy. Mr. X is sick, again, he says. He takes small bites from his sandwich, chews, makes sounds like a kitten, lapping milk. Mr. X is an ancient negro from British Guiana, blind, with deep sunk holes where his eyes are, he took a fall, recently, cracking his face and now his eyes are swelled out, and his cheeks and he looks much younger and healthier. (The androgyne looks like he might molest young boys and hide the bodies behind garages. He brushes his hair all up in front and there're brown spots on his unwashed scalp. And large gapped teeth that've never known a toothbrush.

We take walks in the evening, down to the Exchange for papercups of coke and then to a bench under one of the dark trees. I can't bare to think there's nothing there, but as usual we're reduced to platitudes. Me to stupor. "The grass is green." "The sun's in my eyes." There were a lot of birds on the lawn tonight—the clear yellow of a blackbirds eye. And the mothers, a few benches away, with their plaid plastic bags, waiting for the buses to the Bronx and Queens. "I bring my son grape juice, no, not in a glass, he'll cut his wrists, you know, in a paper cup" (Elixir, mother of waters, healing.) I think of your letter and how you are cultivating your garden. I see it all very clearly. From one of the buildings a patient is screaming, disrupting the quiet neighbor. I try not to listen.

Thursday, July 9

I went to the library today for the first time. It's a rather nice library, a fair number of books and magazines, comfortable chairs, and well-lighted. I saw a collection of Ruth Benedict's work that I'd like to take out, Gogol's Dead Souls that I want to read again; a lot of Eugene O'Neill and the Greeks. I want to read the Greeks, but not yet. Everytime I go into a library I feel so ignorant and ill-read, even tho I read almost all the time. I want to read more of the ancients, I must force myself to read more of the ancients.

Mitch and Denise were up Sunday. Mitch was very good on a dream I had. We had a very disturbing, for me, discussion about the possibility of my being transferred to Ankara, a hospital in N.J. near where my parents live. They think I ought not to go. My parents want me to go. Denise and Mitch think it would be better if I went to a hospital in California, which is where I'm still legally a resident. My dreams tell me to "go to Africa"—meaning the descent and discovery of the dark, fructifying forces of the self. So, you see, it isn't a question of a geographical place outside myself. Anywhere won't be everywhere until I discover the Africa of myself and all that it is.

It's the drink, the man with the blooded face and arms, he told me he knew a way past the custom officials, that he'd been to Africa many times, slipping in roundabout. And I was wildly elated, I had never been to Africa and I begged him to take me, and I will have to follow him roundabout to get in with my valuables intact, declared and revealed, not to them, but to myself.

Denise tells me that you may be coming to NY in the fall. Perhaps somehow I'll be able to see you—I mean I would like that.

Please give best regards to Jess. Later I will have Scribners send you a copy of the book. Oh, and tell Creeley I said hello, that I long to hear from him.

Love to you,
Mike

Outside Rockland at last, Rumaker tried to remember how to live an un-institutionalized life. For inspiration he returned to Duncan, both as symbol and friend. It was to this friend that Rumaker wrote the letter from which Robert Duncan in San Francisco *would grow. Duncan's example was not enough to light his way—Rumaker still had to fight hard and long to gain his own peace of mind—but it was strong enough to guide him, just as Rumaker himself can guide a new generation who seeks to expand the spaces of literary, sexual, and human freedom Rumaker and Duncan first mapped.*

Michael Rumaker to Robert Duncan, January 4, 1961

Dear Robert,

I have re-read your letters, letters I scarcely remember. I had been so withdrawn at Rockland and buried under the river of my life. Now I find them filled with kindnesses I cherish. They are dear to me. But I have always been so troubled by you. This isn't to ask forgiveness in any way but tonight I went to bed and couldn't sleep for thinking of you. I got up and write this now with the moon outside the windows shining on the snow.

Your dark and splendid sensuality has always been foreign to me. I'm a seed feather. Which also has its splendors and toughness. It endures as well. It's only that, not that they are differences but, each is another. It's only that we each, in our own way, work the making of a world.

It's only to say I think of you. However at times mistaken, beneath is a constancy of feeling that remembers your kindness, remembers you as a friend.

Mike

AN INTERVIEW
WITH MICHAEL RUMAKER

Conducted by Ammiel Alcalay and Megan Paslawski

AA: What initially prompted you to write about this period and focus on Robert Duncan?

MR: After I graduated from Black Mountain in 1955, I lived in Philadelphia, and I decided, since several Black Mountain College students had gone on to San Francisco, that I wanted to do that. I ended up hitchhiking across country and got to San Francisco in five or six days and loved the city like everybody does, I think it's America's favorite city, immediately. But then, searching feverishly for a job, I got to see what was going on, the number of *police* that were walking around like storm troopers. Even though there was that marvelous sense of openness, not only about the atmosphere, the climate, that wonderful sense of a peninsular city, being by the sea with open light and the openness of people's attitudes and everyone being so friendly, a lot of artists, writers, musicians, and jazz . . . that there was this undercurrent of fear and homophobia, the police were doing very much what they were doing in New York City, especially then, they were raiding gay bars and raiding gay pads, and putting people in jail.

AA: There's a line in a letter to Duncan, where you write: "you're the richest man in San Francisco," and then you write that San Francisco is "Robert's City." With everything that has gone on in San Francisco, I never heard it put like that.

MR: He was all over the place, his spirit. I don't know about today but certainly then. Very actively involved, and just his presence, and the groups of writers, participating in Joe Dunn's Sunday gatherings when we'd all get together and pass the hat for a gallon of wine, and read poems.

AA: You also have that image of how important the home was, that wall against the world, and in a way that's what he established in the city, the idea of domestic space.

MR: He could live openly and closed. Closed and open, very much like the city itself. Yes, as I was describing it, that sense of openness and closed-ness. We were talking about African Americans and Jews having the family as a refuge, the home, the same certainly was very true for gay people, especially, and gay people living as a couple, two guys living together, as lovers, in a marriage, really, at that time in the 1950s was a pretty scary and brave thing to do. So when I was arrested and dragged into jail, and had to go to court, that was part of the fabric of the whole book, the whole thing of what Duncan was able to avoid, I didn't have that kind of refuge or protection.

AA: Right after that incident, you describe trying to tell the story to John Wieners, and there is a striking passage where you say there was no ground of solidarity to even talk about it.

MR: I was the only one of a group of 20 or 25 men who told Judge Horn, when they asked us to stand and say how we pleaded, I was the only one who stood up and said "Not guilty." And Horn—the judge who dealt with the *Howl* case with Allen Ginsberg, had the sense to say: "case dismissed." The rest all wanted a trial. Now maybe they wanted to air the grievance of being picked up off the street and just arbitrarily arrested for nothing. But that was the closed and oppressive part of the city. Especially for gay people, straight people have no idea, I mean still to this day when they hear about things like that, they can't believe that it happened.

AA: Were there things that you didn't go into that you felt might be too sensitive for Duncan or Jess?

MR: I don't think so. My feeling, as always in my writing, is that when I get squirmy about something, about art, do I dare do this, my good sense says, yeah, you have to, you should, because if it makes you squirm maybe there's a truth there that you need to face, or a fact there that you have to deal with. So I try not to avoid anything, without being sensational.

AA: More of an emotional truth.

MR: Absolutely. You have to really bare yourself; I don't mean you need to bleed at the public wall or something, but you have to be honest to be a writer. It's not the only thing you have to be—like talent helps [laughs], and love of language, the complexities of language—but you do have to be honest, otherwise forget it . . . you can spot dishonesty, don't you think there's a lot of it these days?

AA: How did Duncan react to it?

MR: If you're going to tell the truth, you have to tell the truth about yourself, you really have to be honest about you. You can't just be honest for others. But you also have to be honest about the people you're writing about, and some of it's flattering and some of it's not. And I was very concerned with Robert, knowing his ego, all of us had egos—let's face it—but some had it more than others, and Robert had it in spades. I'll tell you, I mean he was really quite a peacock sometimes. So I was concerned about how he'd take it. It's like treading on someone's story—you have your inner narrative, what you see, what you think is your story, and you don't like it when other people write about you, and as a writer you have to get toughened to that because critics are not going to always be sweetness and light with you in your work. I don't mind attacks on my writing; we don't like them of course, but I don't like *personal* attacks. I don't really know how people really respond to the book. I know one critic wrote that the book, unfortunately, is more about Rumaker than Robert Duncan.

MP: But did you have any more specific indication of how he felt?

MR: Editor Robert Bertholf who, as you know, first published a version of *Robert Duncan in San Francisco* in *Credences* 5/6 (March 1978), was aware of my concern, told me, when he first showed Robert the piece, "Robert only laughed" quite a lot when he read it. That could be taken several ways, of course, but I chose to believe Robert enjoyed it, at least, and that probable rationalization assuaged my worry, even though Robert never told me directly what he thought of it, yea or nay. As I recall, I wrote to Robert, expressing my uneasiness, but he never responded, which I took to mean he wasn't at all that pleased. I believe, from that first publication of *RD in SF* in *Credences*, that I never had any further communication from Duncan. As the old saw goes, silence speaks volumes, and that whatever he had to say about *RD in SF* might only be found in his correspondence with others. Don Allen's Grey Fox Press edition, published in 1996, eight years after Duncan's death, and Don's and my work on that, never evoked from Don, again as I recall, any comments he had heard from Robert on Bertholf's first-version publication.

AA: Have your feelings or your understanding of Duncan changed over the years?

MR: No. Obviously he really is a truly great American poet, I have high respect for that certainly . . . on the personal side, which to me was only interesting because it rounded out the picture, we all have our flaws, and I certainly wrote about mine, in *Black Mountain Days*, or other books, but the main thing is what he accomplished in spite of all *that stuff*. I respected him not only for his genius, and what he did with it, but for his courage at that particular time. He was like one of those beacons, someone to really look forward to, look to and say, well if he can do this so can I. I mean he fed my own gumption to not be destroyed by these homophobes.

That's putting it too bluntly, too simply. Not only as a homosexual but as a writer, as all those things that you were, or are. Duncan didn't get sucked down by that, he didn't get trapped by that. And Olson was certainly another example of the same thing, Olson didn't care what you thought [laughs], it was his vision, and like Duncan's vision, that was the all important thing, and come hell or high water, they were going to achieve that vision in their own work, and obviously they did, certainly Duncan did, certainly Olson did, Creeley, Denise Levertov. . . .

MP: There's a passage where Duncan shows you this picture of himself, young and handsome. . . . Your first reaction is to feel pity and only afterwards you realize this was the most arrogant emotion you could possibly feel for someone who needed to still be seen as this handsome boy.

MR: Yes. He was very beautiful as a young man, and he wasn't ugly or monstrous later, but he wasn't that old when he said that, I think he was in his mid-thirties. You know, it takes time to understand others, one's parents, for instance, or any number of people that you've been close to.

AA: It's an extraordinary passage because as you record your own feelings and respond to the situation, you immediately have to start thinking about what's going through Duncan's mind.

MR: That's what a writer needs to do. If we learn anything from Shakespeare as writers it's to put yourself in the other guy's shoes, the other gal's shoes, that empathy, that ability to transfer. That's a great lesson that needs to be learned, for any human being.

AA: You begin a letter to Duncan that seems to end as a draft of your piece "The Use of the Unconscious." You and Olson were very involved in thinking about dreams, and I wonder if that ever came up with Duncan. It struck me because the image would be: Rumaker the realist and Olson the historian, and you would think questions of the unconscious and myth would be tailor-made for Duncan.

MR: Robert didn't have any influence at that particular time about "The Use of the Unconscious." I think it was finally the accumulation of all my experiences and discussions and listening to Charles talking about Jung and myth and all that big, great, wonderful stew. Melvillian stew, about the unconscious. I can't remember discussing the unconscious or dreams with Duncan, though he would discuss some of his dreams. Charles had tremendous perception, he saw things that I didn't see, mistakes usually, or misperceptions. So he was like a guide, very much like a guide in the dimness of the underworld. And he's often, not lately, but he has for a long time constantly appeared in my dreams. He was always in that dim place. And always seemed to be seated somewhat like a king or on a throne. He'd probably find that funny, but I think it was all the symbology of the language, the night letters of the unconscious, in dreams, and of course, he would always be leaning over my shoulder, and I'd be dreaming that I'm writing and he'd point, like: this is shit.

[laughter] He wouldn't say that in the dream but things like that, you know. He was always criticizing my writing, not always, sometimes they were very friendly dreams. But he was often in that place, it was always dim and it was like one of the visions of Homer's underworld, where he sees his mother in the great swarm. . . . This is quite heady stuff. It was fascinating to me because it was like the idea of the many in the one that Charles certainly ascribed to, after he reheard it from Cornelia Williams, the cook at Black Mountain. I saw it as a very rich source, and the dreams were the budding of that. Your father is presented in the dream being carried on a catafalque, and your father is covered in a golden sheath, like a pharaoh. Where the fuck does that come from? [laughter] Not National Park, New Jersey. [laughter] So you have to pay attention to that, if someone is telling you that, maybe there's something there that you need to see.

AA: In one of the letters you talk about meeting John Wieners at Black Mountain and then later, in San Francisco, and him giving you amphetamines, which you describe like two blue collar Catholics taking the wafer. . . .

MP: With Duncan's resentment lingering in the background [laughter], because he couldn't connect to these Catholics. . . .

MR: Oh yes, yes, because he felt Olson favored John and I . . . the favorite sons. And yes, because Duncan wasn't a Catholic. . . .

AA: It's also kind of obvious, but never really written about, that Olson's "prize" students, you, Ed Dorn, and John Wieners were all working class people.

MR: Yes, Charles always, as you know, had a great empathy. . . . I mean he was working class. So he understood that. But as for John at Black Mountain, he was great fun to be around, and he was just full of energy and just a lively guy and interested in everything. He and those other Boston cronies of his—Joe and Carolyn Dunn, they just devoured everything Olson threw their way, as we all did, but they really devoured it all. John especially. John also, like myself at Black Mountain, discovered once he got through his period of fire, of baptism of fire, that Charles was his mentor too, that he really was the man that he needed to turn to, and John's life was changed, as my life was changed. I mean that was the extraordinary thing about Black Mountain because you could go there looking for what it is you couldn't find anywhere else and if you found it, your life was changed. With John and myself, Olson was really the guy we needed to shake us up and shake us down and get the wax out of the ears . . . [laughter] and the cataracts out of the eyes. Charles never told you what you should do, he didn't want you to write like him, he wanted you to get to the core of yourself. Charles was very good at stripping away all the crap that you came to Black Mountain with, all that you had learned before about writing and he got down to that person, who is you sitting down, and you are conversing with, you are talking, you're talking to somebody, a friend, without all the pretenses of high-flown language and hyperbole . . . but to really get it down, to write as simply as possible, directly as possible, but not to leave out the complexities. So that kind of tightrope walking, that sense of balancing always, so that you get all sides in, to be like Shakespeare, both sides of the character, or many sides of the character, to not leave anything out, to recognize the contradictions that we human beings are filled with, and to not have any ready answers because as the old saying goes—what did Gertrude Stein say? Somebody asked her what is the answer, and she said, "What is the question?"

MP: Despite the huge influence of Olson for you at Black Mountain, was there ever a point where you felt you couldn't take his advice?

MR: Oh yes! Absolutely. What springs to mind immediately is Hart Crane was an anathema in Charles' classes, he just thought Crane was too bound by the strictures of pentameter. But I loved Hart Crane, I still love Hart Crane, the richness of that language, how the *hell* he came up with those *phrases* and the words that suddenly shimmer on the page in a way that no other words do of other poets. That was one instance, and another was Carson McCullers, because he sneered while we were out cutting down the fucking kudzu and it just grows and it grows under your feet as you're cutting it down. And he says, "What are you reading, Rumaker?" and I said, "A Carson McCullers novel," and he said, "Saturday night." [laughter] But I didn't pay any attention to him. I understood what he said about Crane but there was no need for me to tell him about it. Because he probably wouldn't have heard me anyway, he would just say "Well, Michael, someday you'll see."

AA: And how did that work with Duncan, I mean, you didn't have that close of a working relationship?

MR: No, but he was my outside examiner, and he did respect my work. In fact, he even liked my essays on Shakespeare, which surprised me, because I didn't have much respect for them. But he said my writing reminded him of Gogol. And that knocked my socks off, I thought, well, that's pretty good . . . you know, Gogol! [laughter] It was complex with Duncan because of the fact that I wouldn't go to bed with him. He just didn't appeal to me—it's what D.H. Lawrence would call "a sin against the holy ghost." [laughter] You know, if you fuck somebody you don't care about. I think he could be very bitchy about that . . . but that was the personal again, it didn't interfere at all with his great genius, and great ability to write wonderful, mystical poems, which touch you, and give you that sense of being taken somewhere that is very strange and really wonderful, where the mind suddenly is subsumed and the whole body of senses take over and you respond.

AA: Your writing is so *natural*, yet you're always doing something different, so it's very deceptive. It's hard, I think, for a critic to measure that achievement, because you're pushing boundaries constantly.

MR: Duncan called it the conversation with the ideal reader. Something that I learned at Black Mountain, and that

Charles tried to pound in my head, or all of our heads, as writing students, is that writing was like a conversation. Emily Dickinson said it's a love letter, her poems are like love letters to the world, and speaking of Valentine's Day [laughter], those are the best kind, imagine getting a poem from Emily Dickinson . . . but it's like you're talking to someone, and you're having a conversation but it's not a conversation because you the writer are doing the talking, but it's taking the reader, the listener into consideration, that you're talking, as we are talking now, to get that sense into the writing, I think it really draws people in, as you've said, "you feel drawn in." It's getting back to Whitman again too, about "tear the door off the hinges," I can't get that quote right but you know the one I mean, that's really what it is, tear down the barriers, expose yourself, be vulnerable.

AA: How did you feel when you saw "A Poem for Cocksuckers" that later appeared in *The Hotel Wentley Poems* by John Wieners?

MR: Oh, well, god, we shocked each other. [laughter] When I gave a reading at Black Mountain, I read "Exit Three," and John came up to me afterwards, in that way of his, in the soft buttery Bostonian voice, and said "Michael, how'd you have the nerve to write about this marine kissing the narrator in that story?" [laughter] And I thought that was kind of funny, I didn't think the kiss was funny, I just thought John's being so prissy about this baffled me and then when I saw "A Poem for Cocksuckers," I think I saw it in typescript before it was published, I thought "Geez, this guy has really got some balls." [laughter] Well, because that word today is still verboten.

AA: And there's a wonderful letter from Olson to Wieners when he's outraged and writes, "What did they do to 'cocksuckers'?!?!" because the word was censored in the first edition. And Wieners writes back and says, "I'm taking every single copy and I'm writing it in by hand." Of course, in some sense, none of this would be possible without Duncan. It always astonishes me when people first encounter his article "The Homosexual in Society" and realize it was written in 1944, with its extraordinary courage and intelligence. When he writes "Where the Zionists of homosexuality have laid claim to a Palestine of their own, asserting in their miseries, their nationality," he is so prescient.

MR: 1944, it's astonishing.

AA: And you also mention all the women around Duncan, and he tells you how important they are to him.

MP: There's that image when you're laughing about this article in *Life* magazine, with these suburban matrons. . . .

MR: Oh yes. Garden club ladies. . . .

MP: And Duncan has this moment of weird recognition of them in himself and it's impossible for me to read his poetry now without thinking of that. His inner screaming suburban woman. . . .

MR: Yes. His lady of the flowers. There was that sense I think that he had of the female spirit within him, along with the male spirit, that they were conjoined, and I think they are in the best of artists. They have to be, because each has its own strength and its own spirit that feed each other, and make one complete. Duncan had no qualms referring to that aspect of himself. Because what those garden ladies were involved in was the creation of something very beautiful . . . flowers, you know? Duncan's poems very often just blossom before your eyes like that, like he's also the garden club lady who in his poetry just blooms all over the fucking place. . . .

AA: And he had such a recognition of women writers, he rewrites the whole history of modernism through women. . . .

MR: Yes, absolutely. And I remember Anaïs Nin, she recognized that in him, and respected him for it. She also referred to him as a very beautiful young man. And he had great respect for her, she was a very strong woman, Anaïs, to hear her talk, you could hear the strength in her, very direct, very clear sighted, a very beautiful woman. I could see how Duncan would be attracted to her. But it wasn't necessarily that, I think he saw something of the spirit of women that appealed to him and also fed him. And Robert moved very comfortably in his own skin. I think he really was comfortable, very open to life, and it came into him and went out from him.

AA: You have a great portrait of Duncan and Spicer and the respect they had for each other but, again, because you found Spicer so difficult, you have to go through your own experiences to find some empathy for him.

MR: Yes, he was crotchety . . . I really admired his poetry, I really did. But he could be a real son of a bitch. Also because he was really in love with Ebbe Borregaard, and I was screwing Ebbe Borregaard and Ebbe was not screwing Jack Spicer . . . Ebbe was not, I don't think, gay in that sense so I think there was jealousy or something. Also he was an alcoholic. And with my own experiences as an alcoholic, you can be . . . a real negative son of a bitch. Of course they came up through the ranks, both at Berkeley together in the 1940s, so there was that close connection. And Duncan really respected him as a poet. And Spicer certainly respected Duncan.

MP: Because I've been reading through your letters, I wanted to ask about your "Notes from the Asylum." Were they ever published?

MR: The only person who quoted from that was Terry [Leverett T.] Smith, in his book *Eroticizing the Nation*, when I talk about people wanting me to rewrite "The Pipe," other writers and critics wanting me to do that kind of story over and over again. My response from the nuthouse was that I had to be my own self, and I had to write, I couldn't be so restricted, I wanted to try other things, take other chances, other risks, explore other grounds.

AA: In the introduction to a later edition of *Gringos*, Russell Banks writes about people catching up with the tradition in American storytelling that Michael Rumaker seemed so plugged into thirty or more years ago. I think that continues—like when I gave Megan *To Kill a Cardinal.*

MP: I feel like this was a book people were waiting for, if we'd only known. Something Banks said reminded me of what you wrote about Olson telling you, when he said that you were the only one interested in telling a story, everyone else was too "sophisticated," and there was no audience because the audience pretended to be sophisticated.

MR: One always must have in one's writing life the welcome ambush. Where you're going along and thinking—pretty good, I'm writing pretty hot stuff and BOOM, the ambush happens and it's like "wait a minute, what just happened here?" You get thrown off track, you also get thrown out of the rut and are forced into another passage, another tributary, another way. Those ought to be welcome. We don't like them because who likes to be thrown off balance. Anne Waldman has said the same thing, that writing is like shifting the ground. That's not a good paraphrase, but that's what she's saying, and it is true. To learn to walk anew, learn to walk in other directions, in other ways, on ground that is never level.

MP: You seem to have blithely ignored the discrete eras of what people would have considered gay activism in your writing, something that might "date" the work. *To Kill a Cardinal,* for instance, seamlessly weds the spirit of 1970s gay lib and the AIDS activism of the 1980s and early '90s so there is a sense you're a part of the period but also capable of drawing on so much more, in terms of background, in terms of vision. I never felt that things are submerged by their time period as opposed to embracing aspects of it.

MR: I had great fun writing that book. I was asked in an interview why I wrote that book, and I said "pure wickedness." [laughter from all] Because it takes on the Catholic Church. You know, as a former altar boy . . . and really having been a very devout believer as a child. I soon got over that in my teens, my early teens actually. But that whole world that you once felt supported in just came tumbling down. The whole business of using humor to get your point across, it's an old trick. But you have fun and you hope the reader will have fun too. My mother who, for pennies a week, for years and years and years would pay the Prudential insurance man that came around with his big leather book of customers, collecting pennies, so you would get a policy, my mother would have policies on all of her children for the funeral in case they died, because if you didn't have any money, where would you go? Bury you in a pauper's grave or put you out with the trash or something . . . and so when she died these policies were cashed in by my oldest brother, and we each got three thousand or thirty-five hundred dollars, something like that, and that enabled me to publish *To Kill a Cardinal* . . . [laughter from all] Little did she know. . . .

MP: What did your family think?

MR: They don't say anything, if they indeed read it. My sister-in-law, who was a nun, she read it, and thought it was a hoot. And she's a very devout Catholic, but she has a sense of humor, thank goodness. So I don't think my mother would have liked it at all, she had a sense of humor, but not that kind of sense of humor. [laughter from all] But you're right, I meant it as a satire, and there is something delicious about using satirical writing, but satire is the refuge of the powerless, so you might as well have a good time using it because it's the only power you have, to make fun of those authority figures that are stupid or pompous. And it's an old way to do things.

AA: You've never been fully recognized or embraced in what gets codified as gay writing; what do you think the root of that is?

MR: I was thinking that maybe it boils down to I just haven't kissed enough ass. And also there's an element of, do you do a lot of reviews, do you do the "one hand washes the other" kind of thing in the literary world. . . .

AA: I also think it's a bigger problem with prose writers, since so many of the great prose writers of your generation are hardly read—Douglas Woolf, even Hubert Selby. It seems as much of a formal issue as an identity issue, that a lot of people might just not understand where your writing is coming from. Speaking of ambushes, I was reading a letter you wrote to Joanne Kyger, where you talk about first meeting Allen Ginsberg and Peter Orlovsky, after you'd written that critique of *Howl* that appeared in *Black Mountain Review*, and how Ginsberg actually appreciated the piece.

MR: You had to bring up *Howl*!

AA: You paint a pretty grim picture of the options: "university is out of the question, the other asylums state nut house reform school psycho wards grey hand of care won't do not the necessary atmosphere." [laughter]

MR: Oh my god . . . the voice of the past! It was 1957, that's when I first met Allen and Peter. We were staying at Denise Levertov and Mitch Goodman's place. Allen told me that when he read the review in *The Black Mountain Review*, over in Tangier with Peter, he spent many a night arguing with me before he fell off to sleep. [laughter] Oh that poor guy, what I put him through! [laughter] That's just terrible, you know. But he did say that I treated it fairly, he used some phrase that was mitigating. . . . My experience with Allen was that he was fair, he sort of had a buoyancy about him, and we became very good friends and he didn't hold grudges.

AA: You mention Denise Levertov again. In the correspondence between Duncan and Levertov, people tend to forget that when they talked about a "new book" in the 1950s it was often a carbon copy typescript making its way from friend to friend. In *Black Mountain Days* you describe the thrill of Olson getting a letter from Duncan with a new poem in it and reading it to the class.

MR: It was like the Russians, samizdat. That was really very, very exciting. To have letters, getting poems hot off the type-writer from Duncan or Creeley or any number of people. We didn't have mimeograph machines, there were no computers, no copying machines . . . you just had carbon paper and things just circulated like that.

AA: Can you say something more about Levertov, there seems to have been a lot of kindness from her towards you during difficult times.

MR: Oh, absolutely, yes. Denise was dealing with my mother, my mother and father because I was just incapable of dealing with anything. I had no place to go when Donald Allen took me to the Psychiatric Institute in upper Manhattan. I needed to be some place where I was safe. And she was there, and Don was too. Don said later he was sorry he had ever gotten mixed up in it. It seemed like it was quite a burden, which I could certainly understand, and just made me feel so guilty. But there was nothing I could do. It was silly to blame myself, deep depression, clinical depression makes you helpless, you are up against walls that you can't climb over, you can't get through, you can't do anything. So I felt very bad about that I put so many people through such discomfort, and concern, my mother especially, my parents. But there was nothing I could do really, nothing I could do. And it's a mystery—if it is a chemical disease then you can't blame yourself. But she was very wonderful, I think the nurse came out in her, you know she had been a nurse in England. And she was really a great help.

AA: Where did you first meet her?

MR: It had to be in Manhattan, and it had to be in the gatherings of poets and writers. Yes, because then I stayed, they invited me to stay at their apartment while they were off in Maine for several months. And I was in pretty bad shape then. She wasn't very active socially. She was really annoyed when I think she met Ginsberg and Peter for the first time in somebody's apartment, and the both of them took down their pants and pissed in the fireplace. [laughter] I mean, Don, he could be really nasty. He thought she was awfully priggish about that, I mean after all, you don't mind, you wouldn't mind if your guests came and pissed in your fireplace, would you? [laughter]

MP: I've had guests do similar . . . [laughter] And were you in touch with Levertov later as you became more activist-oriented? There was a point where it seemed like there was some kind of anxiety with her not siding with Duncan over something.

MR: Yes, about *The Butterfly*. Duncan, quite rightly, said that the ending of *The Butterfly*, that novel of mine, was mawkish, sentimental, and he didn't like it. And she defended *The Butterfly*. I went to see her read at St. Marks because I wanted to see her again, and when the reading was over I went up and talked with her. She too said she hated to do what she had to do about getting me into a mental hospital. And I just told her she shouldn't have felt that way because I was glad that she helped. They all felt very guilty which made me feel extremely guilty that I caused everybody so much discomfort. How glibly I talk about that time in my life . . . when I think about it, somebody should write a biography of this guy. [laughter] I mean, when you think back, I'm sure both of you two, well, when you get to be eighty you think back on it, you say, "Jesus Christ how did I survive so much of this stuff?" And I just say that as a fact, just looking back at so many stupid things that I sort of got involved in: alcoholism, drug addiction, depression, schizophrenia, and oh, and then writing! [laughter] That's what it takes, I guess, to be a writer. Maybe that's a rather romantic notion, but I think it does help. I think D.H. Lawrence was right, you know, you don't know the tops unless you know the bottoms. I think we do need to have that full dimension of ourselves, of what it is to be human. It's not all moonlight and roses and sunshine-y days. We can't avoid the dark side. We have to look at that . . . that's the most painful thing. So we earn our way, we earn our way, the right to words that speak the truth, hard earned truths.

MP: I was hoping you'd tell us a bit about your memories of the March on Washington in 1979.

MR: Do I talk about the buildings in Washington looking like mausoleums to me? And being amongst people who are not going to bop you over the head, or throw you in jail? It's the way blacks feel amongst each other, the way LeRoi Jones, when he talked about how he loved and missed so much, the Negro baseball leagues and going to the games in Newark with his father. And being amongst black folk, all black folk.

MP: When I was sitting in the archive reading this I felt a surge of recognition. For the first time I was really in a crowd like that. . . .

MR: And it was joyous, it was celebratory like the Pride marches. . . . I remember that letter to Don, and I think I felt very high, the good feeling that was generated by that march. That's why public activism is really very important, once you go, once the private face becomes a public face it becomes a protest against an injustice, it's very freeing. As you move towards the eccentric, from the eccentric to the centric, then you can see back into the centric and see what a bunch of bullshit a lot of it is. It's to have those eyes. The oppressors are very blind to a lot of things that a lot of heterosexuals don't see and that homosexuals see very clearly. You really learn to be alert, if anybody is coming after you. I was referring to homosexuals and women, and everybody who has been persecuted and oppressed, when somebody's coming after you, you learn to see an awful lot about them, to get a sense of danger when you know they get too near. And very often you didn't know who the hell your enemies were, you didn't know who you were talking to, you didn't know who was a homophobe, a very dangerous one, that could beat you up or kill you. So it was important to be alert and sharp and on your toes and know who was who and what was what. And to trust the gut.

AA: Here we are in 2012, and you've recently turned 80. You've been through all this, no matter how glibly you put it, I don't think it's very glib the way you've written it. What do you feel is most important to transmit, to convey now?

MR: I don't know if I can really answer that. I do know that I felt a very strong conviction sitting on the steps of the Nyack Library, next door to where we had lunch today, one sunny morning, and thinking about my writing, and this had to be the early seventies, and deciding that I would henceforth try to write some things that might in a way help others not to go through what I went through. And I chose to write in the first person singular, to really just write, you know: not me, me—not really in an egoistic way. So the outcome was *A Day and a Night at the Baths*, and that was a freeing experience. That was something I wasn't ready to do when I was transitioning from Black Mountain to San Francisco, when you could get thrown in jail and it was against the law to be queer. The poisons of the atmosphere, no matter where you went in America, there were always possible enemies who were out to get you. And I think that clearing, so the poisons are out there but as a result there's also poison within you, within your own head. So writing, I don't mean writing as therapy, but it certainly was a cleansing of the spirit. A burning away, a burning away of all that stuff that was poisoning *me* from within. And I thought then maybe if I write about this and honestly do that, openly—because sometimes you can read something and it sticks with you for life. Mary Fiore said that about Charles, that he'd say things that stuck to you like adhesive tape, that you didn't understand at the time but only understood years later. "I would remember things that he said and I didn't quite know what the hell he was talking about but they stuck with me." And then later, you know, like decades later she'd say "Oh! Ta-da!" So it doesn't matter when people get it, so long as *you* get it and then get it out.

AA: When Diane di Prima visited my class once, students were reading *Recollections of My Life as a Woman* and somebody asked, "How could you write such emotional things?" And she said, "This isn't emotional, I wrote this to tell people, particularly young women, what I went through so that they might learn something. And not go through it themselves."

MR: Yes, yes, absolutely. That's the true usefulness of shared experience. And it may not save anyone, we can't save anyone from their own experience, but if you're having a lot of really poisonous trouble, maybe hearing something will start that cleansing process.

Biographical Notes

MICHAEL RUMAKER, a son first of blue-collar Philadelphia and later New Jersey, was born in 1932. His hometowns provided the material for several important works such as *Pagan Days* (1999) and "Exit 3" (1967). Rumaker graduated in 1955 from Black Mountain College, for him a stronghold of literary inspiration and friendship. He earned an MFA from Columbia University in 1970. Rumaker's fiction includes *The Butterfly* (1962), *Gringos and Other Stories* (1967), *A Day and a Night at the Baths* (1979), *My First Satyrnalia* (1981), and *To Kill a Cardinal* (1992). His memoir *Black Mountain Days,* a lovingly detailed exploration of his writerly apprenticeship, appeared in 2003. City Lights' expanded reprint of *Robert Duncan in San Francisco* partakes in a groundswell of new interest in Rumaker's work. Recent years have seen the publication of new editions of *Black Mountain Days, A Day and a Night at the Baths,* and Leverett T. Smith Jr.'s *Eroticizing the Nation: Michael Rumaker's Fiction,* along with *Selected Letters.* His archive at the Thomas J. Dodd Research Center of the University of Connecticut officially opened in April 2012. Rumaker taught creative writing at The New School for Social Research, SUNY—Buffalo, and City College—CUNY. He continues to live and write in Nyack, NY.

AMMIEL ALCALAY'S recent books are *a little history* and a new edition of *from the warring factions*. City Lights has published *Memories of Our Future* (1999), various translations, and a novel, *Islanders* (2010). *"neither wit nor gold" (from then)*, came out in 2011. He teaches at Queens College and the Graduate Center of the City University of New York, and is the general editor of *Lost & Found: The CUNY Poetics Document Initiative*.

MEGAN PASLAWSKI, a graduate of McGill University and Trinity College Dublin, is currently a doctoral student in English Literature at the Graduate Center of the City University of New York. Her collection of selected letters by Michael Rumaker, *like a great armful of wild & wonderful flowers*, appeared from *Lost & Found* in the spring of 2012. She lives in Brooklyn and teaches writing and literature at Queens College.

Acknowledgments

Our heartfelt thanks to Michael Rumaker, for his humor, openness, generosity, and confidence in our ability to present his work as he would like to see it presented. Thanks to Elaine Katzenberger and Garrett Caples for their willingness to explore this project and their commitment to taking it on. On the archival side, both Rumaker and Duncan have been blessed with conscientious and enthusiastic guardians: Melissa Watterworth Batt (Curator of Literary, Natural History and Rare Books Collections), and the entire staff at the Thomas J. Dodd Research Center at the University of Connecticut, always offered invaluable help; our thanks to them are ongoing. With the official opening of the Michael Rumaker Papers at the Dodd Center, we know this resource will continue to reveal further treasures and would recognize here, as well, the foresight and dedication of the late George Butterick. We could not have proceeded without the good graces of Jim Maynard and Mike Basinski at The Poetry Collection of the University Libraries, University at Buffalo, The State University of New York, where our queries are always met with intelligence, wit, and speed. It was Jim who found the extraordinary cover photo of Duncan, taken by Helen Adam. Thanks to Lisa Jarnot, author of the new Duncan biography, who originally suggested where we might look for a period photo. Nor could we have published some of this material without the blessings of Christopher Wagstaff and Mary Margaret Sloan, trustees of the Jess Collins Trust. Thanks as well to Peter Quartermain, general editor of *The Collected Writings of Robert Duncan*, for continuing help. We would, as well, like to posthumously acknowledge the extraordinary work of Donald Allen (1912-2004), ranging from his time at Grove Press to editor and publisher of the Writing Series, Four Seasons Foundation, and Grey Fox Press. Allen not only introduced new writing to a wider public but kept important work (documents, essays, interviews, and other extra-poetic materials) in circulation. His achievement was enormous and *Lost & Found* owes much to his spirit. At the CUNY Graduate Center: to all our colleagues in the Ph.D. Program in English, particularly Profs. Mario DiGangi and Carrie Hintz for their support; and to the Doctoral Students' Council and Center for the Humanities for travel and research opportunities. On the *Lost & Found* side, thanks and gratitude, always, to Aoibheann Sweeney, Director of the Center for the Humanities. Able to leap tall administrative hurdles in a single bound, she is our superhero without whom *Lost & Found* would simply not be possible. To the rest of the dedicated, tireless, and always spirited staff at the Center who provide constant support: Ana Božičević, Sampson Starkweather, and Tonya Foster: thanks! Michael Seth Stewart, editor of the *John Wieners & Charles Olson: Selected Correspondence* and further John Wieners projects, offered invaluable support along the way. Lauren Baggett's insight is always appreciated. Thanks to Maryam Parhizkar for pinpoint proofreading. Finally, Amber Snider answered the call for quick and accurate transcription, both of the interview and some of the letters; our gratitude is boundless!

LOST & FOUND / LOST & FOUND ELSEWHERE

LOST & FOUND: The CUNY Poetics Document Initiative publishes primary sources by figures associated with New American Poetry in an annual series of chapbooks under the general editorship of Ammiel Alcalay. Lost & Found's aim is to open the field of inquiry and illuminate the terrain of an essential chapter of twentieth-century letters. The series has published little-known work by Amiri Baraka, Diane di Prima, Robert Duncan, Langston Hughes, Frank O'Hara, Margaret Randall, Muriel Rukeyser, and many others.

Under the auspices of The Center for the Humanities, and with the guidance of an extended scholarly community, Lost & Found chapbooks are researched and prepared by students and guest fellows at the PhD Program in English of the Graduate Center of the City University of New York. Utilizing personal and institutional archives, Lost & Found scholars seek to broaden our literary, cultural, and political history.

LOST & FOUND ELSEWHERE is a unique new series of book-length projects emerging from this research. Working in partnership with select publishers, these books bring to light unpublished or long unavailable materials that have emerged alongside or as part of the Lost & Found project. Available in this series:

Robert Duncan in San Francisco **Michael Rumaker** Expanded edition, with selected correspondence and interview edited by Ammiel Alcalay and Megan Paslawaski CITY LIGHTS PUBLISHERS	*A Walker in the City: Elegy for Gloucester* **Peter Anastas** With an afterword by Ammiel Alcalay BACK SHORE PRESS	*Savage Coast* **Muriel Rukeyser** Edited, with an introduction by Rowena Kennedy-Epstein THE FEMINIST PRESS

For more information, visit lostandfoundbooks.org